KNITTING PATTERNS FROM NATURE

· CAROLYN HARRIS ·

B.T. Batsford Ltd · London

My sincere thanks to Angela Corby, Joan Woodhouse, Mahala Trevaldwyn and Bryden Henderson; and to Andrew Grant-Adamson for colour photographs 4, 6, 7 and 8, and Richard Bird for colour photographs 1, 2, 3 and 5.

ISBN 0 7134 5703 1

Typeset by Servis Filmsetting Ltd, Manchester

Printed in Great Britain by Anchor Press, Tiptree, Essex

for the publishers B.T. Batsford Ltd
4 Fitzhardinge Street, London W1H 0AH

CONTENTS

PREFACE

This book has been written for the reader who has already mastered the basics of creative knitting and who now wants to produce beautiful and original knitwear. The designs are for both hand and machine knitters.

The shapes of nature are wonderful, and seem perfect in design – from the vigorous shoots and buds of spring and the tranquil summer flowers, to the frosty, skeleton shapes of winter. All the designs were inspired by nature, and reflect the changing seasons and the varied flora and fauna of the countryside. The designs began as sketches, which were then reduced to geometric outlines, suitable for knitting patterns. As the presentation follows the seasons through the year, the knitter is shown how to produce seasonally-appropriate garments.

All the design processes are carefully explained and clearly illustrated. The reader is shown how to produce each design; how to make changes to alter the shape; how to alter the design with decorative effects, and how to experiment with the pattern and stitches for a more individually expressive design.

The basic shapes are extremely simple; all the techniques involved are clearly explained, and demonstrated in accompanying line drawings. Extra interest comes from the fact that many other forms of craft work are incorporated within the designs, such as appliqué and embroidery.

This book gives many suggestions for different projects which can be produced from one pattern, giving beginners and experts alike encouragement through self-criticism, visual appreciation, awareness of what is around, and a stimulus through nature. This teaches a great deal about yarns and the problems that the knitter sometimes comes across: colour, texture, stitches and patterns, fabric, and proportion of design.

INTRODUCTION

Those readers who are very experienced knitters might find this introductory text a useful way of refreshing their memories on particular points. Less-certain knitters should read the explanations before starting to knit, and should refer back from the patterns as often as is useful.

· TENSION ·

Before starting to knit one of the designs, it is important to check whether your tension is the same as given in the pattern. Tension often differs with each knitter, but don't worry about it too much: the shapes of the designs involve few calculations, so if your tension is different, it will simply mean changing needles to try to fit the tension.

On the other hand, you could ignore the tension given in the pattern, knit your own tension sample and measure it, then work out your own pattern, simply knitting to the measurements of the design.

First of all, whether it is a hand or machine knit, you must knit a tension sample using the needles and yarn in the pattern.

Machine knitters should follow the usual methods used for knitting a tension sample.

Hand knitters should knit up a sample of at least 12cm (4¾in) square. The tension for each design is given as the number of stitches and rows to 10cm (4in), so your sample should be a bit bigger to make it easier for you to measure.

Should your square have more stitches or rows than given in the pattern, this means that you knit a little more tightly, so try using larger needles on the same number of stitches. If your square has fewer stitches or rows than stated, it means that you knit a bit looser, so try a smaller pair of needles on the same number of stitches.

· COLOUR ·

Don't feel too tied to the colours given in the patterns. You can send for colour charts for the various yarns, and then choose your own from the selection; but don't forget to check your tension carefully, as this can differ with each colour, even though it is the same yarn.

· PATTERN NOTES ·

Before you start knitting, read any pattern notes carefully so that you understand everything about the pattern before you start. It is taken for granted that you understand the basic theory of hand and machine knitting, though any special techniques are explained.

Mark with a pen all the instructions for the size you want to knit, as this will make the pattern much easier to follow. A highlighter pen could be particularly useful here.

· MACHINES ·

Don't be discouraged from trying a pattern if you don't have that particular make of machine (if it is a machine knitting design). Use your own machine's facilities and just keep to the overall shape.

For machine knitters without punchcards, try to see the punchcard pattern given as a means of doing a different kind of patterning. After all, a hole to be punched to be knitted in the contrast yarn could just as well represent where to position your French knots, if one blank hole equals one French knot.

· YARNS ·

As many of the yarns used are natural fibres, be careful to read the yarn band thoroughly. They will need to be hand-washed with care, usually in warm rather than hot water. You should not wring wet garments but rather pat them gently in to place.

Knitted fabric should never be ironed, that is, have an iron passed backwards and forwards over it; this will distort the fabric and push the stitches out of place. If it does need a press, place the iron (preferably a steam one) on the garment, then lift it up and replace on another part of the garment, and repeat until it has all been pressed. A Teflon (or other) iron cover will protect the wool from overheating.

The quantities of yarn required for a certain pattern err on the generous side, because it is much better to have too much of a yarn, rather than too little.

Should you be unable to obtain yarns as specified in the patterns, purchase a similar thickness and type of wool, and experiment with various needle sizes until you obtain the correct tension.

· FINISHING OFF ·

Although it is not mentioned for individual patterns, all the ends must be neatly darned in at the back or sides of the work. Use a tapestry needle, and thread each end in turn, sewing them in for a few centimetres before cutting them off.

· PRESSING ·

Before sewing up your garment, and if the yarn can bear heat, you should press each piece separately (see under *Yarns* above). To save distorting the knitting, fold each piece in half, right sides inside, and keeping the sides level. Pin the double section to the ironing board and press as usual, avoiding the centre fold. You can press the centre later on the wrong side.

· SEWING UP ·

Most knitters have their own favourite methods of sewing up their work. It helps always to follow the same routine, that is, to sew up in the same order each time. It is also better to sew the pieces before washing the garment, as you would with Shetland knitting, for instance, as the fabric is firmer before it is washed.

Three methods of sewing up are described below.

· Flat seam ·

This is used mostly for ribbing, or for joining pieces knitted in chunky or textured yarns. (If the garment is knitted in a very thick wool, it is best to divide it into separate strands for sewing up.)

Match the edges of knitting, right sides together, and secure the end of the sewing-up yarn with a backstitch. Take the needle backwards and forwards through the edge stitches, making a line of running stitches.

· Backstitch seam ·

This is suitable for armholes, raglan and shoulder seams.

Match the edges of the work, with right sides together, and secure the sewing-up yarn at the right-hand edge of the seam. Bring the yarn through on the seam line, then take a small backward stitch through the knitting. Bring the needle through again a little in front of the first stitch; take another stitch, inserting the needle at the point where it first came through.

· Invisible seam ·

This is most suitable for joining straight-sided pieces knitted in stocking stitch.

Secure the sewing yarn at the bottom of the seam on the right-hand piece. With the right sides of both pieces of work facing you, pass the needle across to the other side of the work, pick up one stitch and pull the yarn through. Pass the needle across the back to the first side of the work, pick up one stitch and pull the yarn through. Continue along the seam, making rungs across from one piece to the other, and pulling each stitch up tightly; this will give a lovely finish as the sewing is truly invisible on the right side of the work.

If you sew the seams of the garment on a sewing machine, use a strong thread of slightly deeper tone to your yarn. Use Drima or Guttermann's polyester thread.

When sewing the seam of a section to be turned back (like the roll-back collar on the silver birch design) remember to sew that part on the reverse side. Sew the seam as usual to 2cm (¾in) of the part to be turned back, then sew the remainder on the right side, as this will be the wrong side in wear.

I always cut a length of cotton tape to the measurement

from one sleeve top to the opposite one; this goes along one shoulder seam, behind the back of the neck, and along the other shoulder seam. On a dropped-sleeve garment, this will be the width of the top of the garment front. The strength of this cotton tape ensures that the sweater keeps its shape.

ABBREVIATIONS

The following abbreviations are used within the garment patterns.

alt	alternate(ly)
approx	approximate(ly)
beg	begin(ning)
carr	carriage
cm	centimetre(s)
CO	cast off
col	colour
COn	cast on
cont	continue
dec	decreas(e), (ing)
ev	every
foll	follow(s), (ing)
g	gramme(s)
HP	holding position
in	inch(es)
inc	increas(e), (ing)
K	knit
mm	millimetre(s)
MT	main tension
MY	main yarn
NWP	non-working position
opp	opposite
oz	ounce(s)
P	purl
patt	pattern
PC	punchcard
r(s)	row(s)
rem	remaining
rep	repeat
RS	right side(s)
sl	slip
st(s)	stitch(es)
st st	stocking stitch
T	tension
tog	together
WK	waste knitting
WP	working position
WS	wrong side(s)
WY	waste yarn

Please note that measurements shown in the diagrams do not have 'cm' and 'in' following them, in order to make the illustrations as clear as possible. Following the text style, centimetres are always printed first, followed by inches.

NEEDLE SIZES

British	American	Metric
14	00	2mm
13	0	$2\frac{1}{4}$mm
12	1	$2\frac{3}{4}$mm
11	2	3mm
10	3	$3\frac{1}{4}$mm
9	4	$3\frac{3}{4}$mm
8	5	4mm
7	6	$4\frac{1}{2}$mm
6	7	5mm
5	8	$5\frac{1}{2}$mm
4	9	6mm
3	10	$6\frac{1}{2}$mm
2	11	7mm
1	12	$7\frac{1}{2}$mm
0	13	8mm
00	14	9mm
000	15	10mm

BRITISH AND AMERICAN TERMS

British	American
Stocking stitch (st st)	Stockinette stitch (st st)
Tension	Gauge
Increase 1	Make 1
Cast off	Bind off
Catch down	Tack down
Double crochet	Single crochet
Swiss darning	Duplicate stitch
Wool round needle (wrn)	Yarn over needle (y.o)
Yarn forward	Yarn over or yarn to front

Yarns

British	American
4-ply	Sport
Double knitting	Knitting worsted
Aran-weight	Fisherman
Chunky	Bulky

SPRING

1 The countryside welcomes the spring

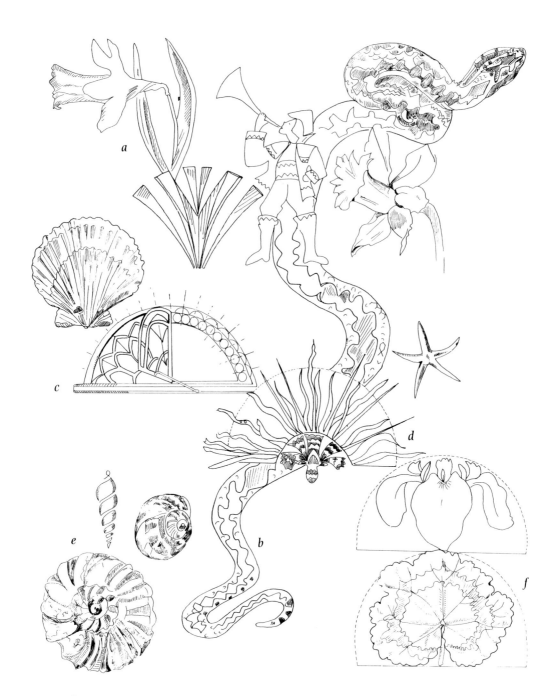

2 Shapes from nature with a very vigorous outline
  a) The daffodil with its trumpet-shaped head
  b) The compelling curves of a snake
  c) The uplifting shape of a shell or an arch
  d) The radiating sun
  e) Special shapes of shells
  f) Shapes of flowers and leaves

Springtime in the country is when everything seems to wake up and come alive again after winter. Spring corn is sewn, to be harvested in August; new shoots and buds are growing, and new-born lambs are in the fields (*Fig 1*).

The daffodil is one of the first flowers in the spring, with its welcoming trumpet-shaped face.

The shapes from nature at this time seem very vigorous and dynamic (*Fig 2*).

All outlines can be reduced to a geometric shape. For the knitter who is looking either for a pattern that she can repeat, or for an attractive outline to use for a decorative effect, the most simple form of a shape is the easiest to cope with. You can see from the sketches how this evolves (*Fig 3*).

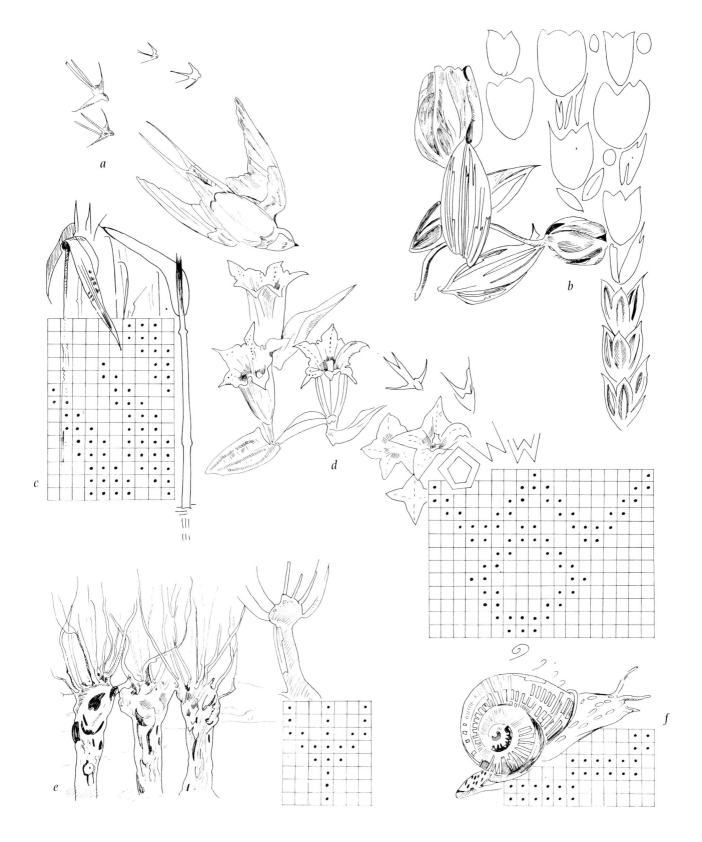

3 How a pattern evolves from a sketch to a geometric outline
  a) The two tail feathers of a swallow give a forceful outline
  b) Tulips radiate cheerfulness
  c) Upright reeds suggest stability
  d) Willow gentians are also cheerful
  e) Pollarded trees have an uplifting outline
  f) The eye is drawn to the shape of the snail

SILVER BIRCH
· machine-knitted jumper ·

The idea for the design of this jumper came from seeing the bark of the silver birch tree. The cable pattern on the welt and cuffs looks, at a distance, like ears of corn, and I combined the two patterns to make the design (*Figs 4, 5 and 6*).

If you reduce an outline of corn, either wheat or barley,

4 Silver birch jumper – design sketch

Neck

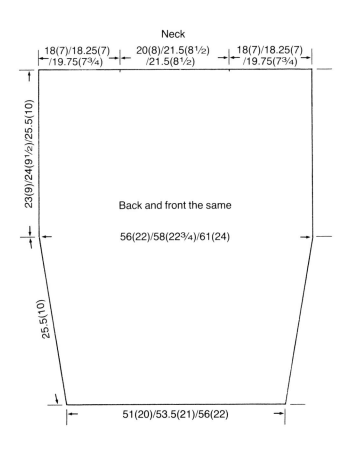

18(7)/18.25(7)/19.75(7¾)   20(8)/21.5(8½)/21.5(8½)   18(7)/18.25(7)/19.75(7¾)

23(9)/24(9½)/25.5(10)

Back and front the same

56(22)/58(22¾)/61(24)

25.5(10)

51(20)/53.5(21)/56(22)

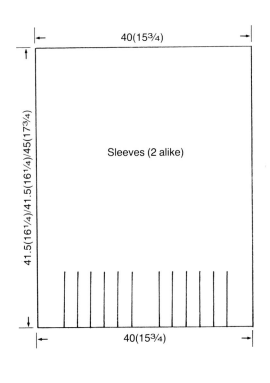

40(15¾)

41.5(16¼)/41.5(16¼)/45(17¾)

Sleeves (2 alike)

40(15¾)

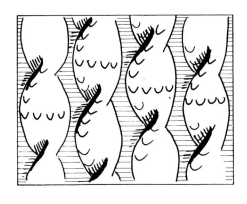

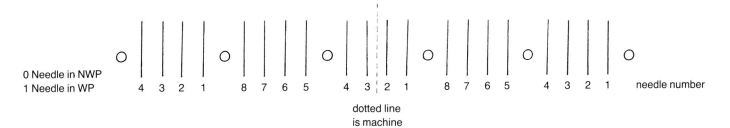

0 Needle in NWP
1 Needle in WP

4 3 2 1   8 7 6 5   4 3 | 2 1   8 7 6 5   4 3 2 1   needle number

dotted line
is machine
centre 0

5 *Silver birch measurements Cable pattern shown in detail*
Needle set-up for cable pattern

13

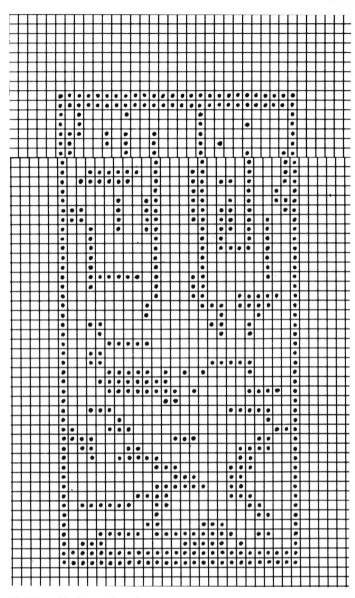

6 Silver birch punchcard

beads, and leather thonging over knitted cord is used as a belt. Fringing on the trousers, with threaded wooden beads, complements the jumper.

· THE DESIGN ·

Beautifully soft yarns are used together to knit this loose-fitting, cropped jumper. It is machine-knitted using a punchcard inspired by the bark on a silver birch tree. Wonderful colours and textures are blended together.

The jumper has a roll-back collar and is decorated with wooden beads. The slightly-shaped body is gathered into an easy-to-do cabled welt, which is buttoned at the middle front, and can be drawn in by ties that meet at both the back and front.

There is an unusual smocking in leather thonging on the sleeves; they are gathered into a loose cuff which has the same cable stitch and button panel as the welt.

· SIZES ·

To fit 81–86(91–96, 101)cm, 32–34(36–38, 40)in bust.

· MATERIALS ·

Yarns are from Texere.

440(500, 540)g, 16(17¾, 19½) oz 50% wool, 50% silk, off-white, shade 286, col A

50g (2oz) pure alpaca, each, beige, dark brown, taupe, light mauve, pink, cinnamon brown, light blue, and dark blue, shade 296, 4-ply equivalent

7 diamond-shaped pearl buttons

Leather thonging and wooden beads, natural col

Cotton tape

· TENSION ·

32 sts and 30 rs to 10cm (4in) measured over PC patt (T9 approx)

to a geometric shape, you could see it as a row of squares. I threaded three square beads in a natural wood colour on a piece of the background colour yarn, and then sewed them in a random spacing over the front of the jumper.

Various ways of wearing the silver birch jumper are shown in Fig 7.

If you knitted the shape of silver birch in Shetland wool, in stripes of green and red, you could achieve a plaid effect by adding vertical and horizontal lines in a contrast colour in chain stitch. Add a knitted pocket and detached chainstitch flowers. There is a raised seam effect on the top of the ribbed sleeves (*Fig 7a*).

A short hand-knitted jacket in a very textured stitch pattern would look ideal worn over this silver birch jumper (*Fig 7b*). The design on the jumper is picked out in pearls or

7 Silver birch and acorn slipover – various ways of adding
decorative effects – a) raised seam; b) textured stitch jacket; c)
scrolling at the opening; d) belted and worn with bomber jacket

Silver Birch

· MACHINES ·

This pattern is suitable for standard gauge punchcard machines.

· PATTERN NOTES ·

Punch card before starting to knit. Body pieces are knitted in pattern punchcard. Use the punchcard on the sleeves, but lock it on certain rows for an elongated effect. There is a cable pattern on welt and cuffs, which is detailed within the pattern.

· PATTERN COLOUR CHANGE ·
· SEQUENCE ·

(Unless you have a multi-colour change tension mast, arrange contrast colours on floor at front of machine, and, without breaking the yarn just used, remove it and then thread the new yarn through the carriage yarn feeder.)

Yarn A in feeder 1 throughout, changing contrast cols in feeder 2 as follows:

4 rs pale blue
4 rs dark blue
4 rs dark brown
4 rs dark blue
4 rs pale blue
2 rs beige
2 rs cinnamon
2 rs taupe
2 rs mauve
2 rs pink
2 rs mauve
2 rs taupe
12 rs cinnamon

· BACK AND FRONT (the same) ·

Insert PC and lock on starter r (r 8 for Brother KH 830). Push 164(170, 180) ns to B position, then pull out alt ns to E position. COn 'e' loop method on these ns. T7, and yarn A, K to left. K to right (all ns now in WP), K to left.

Set machine to K Fair Isle. K to right. RC000. T9. Release

card, commence col sequence and patt. *At the same time,* inc 1 st at each end of rs 9, 18, 27, 36, 45, 54, 63 and 72. 180(186, 196) sts. K straight to r 76. Mark both ends of r.

Cont in patt and col sequence to RC144(148, 152) (patt finishes on 2nd r of dark blue). Mark st 58(59, 63) from both edges of work (for neck). Release on several rs of WK.

· SLEEVES (2 alike) ·

Push up 128 ns to WP. COn with WY and K several rs. RC000. T7, yarn A, K straight in st st to RC30. Mark centre 0 n with length of contrast yarn.

To prepare knitting for smocking effect later: on ns 5, 10, 15, 20, 25 and 30 to left of centre 0, and on the same ns to right of centre 0, release the st and allow to run down to first line of knitting in A. Catch st with safety pin. N stays in NWP. T9, yarn A, K straight to RC33(33, 43). Carr at left. Insert PC and lock so machine will commence patt on r 24 of patt.

Set machine to K Fair Isle. K to right. *Dark brown in feeder 2. Release PC. Patt for 8 rs. Change contrast yarn to taupe. Set card lock lever to double length patterning. Patt for 20 rs*.

Lock card. Change contrast yarn to mauve. Patt for 32 rs. RC94(94, 104). Rep from * to *, changing cols as before. RC122(122, 132).

Set machine to K plain. K 2 rs in yarn A. CO. RC124(124, 134).

· WELT ·

COn over 24 ns in yarn A. Carr on left.

· Button band ·

T7, yarn A, K 6 rs.
K 1 r at T10 (folding r).
K 6 rs at T7. Carr at right. RC000. T9. Transfer sts for cable patt (Diag 1).

Cable patt n set-up: transfer 3rd and ev foll 5th st onto adjacent n at left and right of centre 0. Push empty ns to NWP. K to left.

· Welt facing ·

Leave n 13 on left in NWP, then COn over next 20 ns (ns 14 to 33). K to right.

*K 4 rs. Cross sts 1 and 2 in front of sts 3 and 4 (i.e. lift sts 1 and 2 onto double transfer tool, move sts 3 and 4 onto ns 1 and 2, then place sts 1 and 2 onto ns 3 and 4). Pull crossed sts to E position (to make it easier for the machine). K 4 rs. Cross sts 5 and 6 in front of sts 7 and 8. Again, pull crossed sts to E position. These 8 rs from * form one patt.

K in patt until RC388. Bring ns in NWP to WP. T7, K to left. CO 20 sts for welt facing. On remaining 24 sts, rep button band. CO.

· CUFFS (*2 alike*) ·

COn the same number of sts and K as for welt cable patt and facing with button bands, but complete cable patt over 90 rs.

· DRAWSTRING CORDS (*2 alike*) ·

COn over 3 sts. T9 and yarn A. Push in one part button. K in st st for 504 rs. CO.

· ROLL-BACK COLLAR ·

Join left shoulder seam. Push 128(136, 136) ns into WP. RC000. WS of work facing, replace 64(68, 68) sts from both back and front neck onto ns. Bring 1n up at both edges, 130(138, 138) sts. Pull ns to E position. RC000. T9 and yarn A, K 1 r.
T7, K 7 rs.
T8, K 4 rs.
T9, K 12 rs. RC24.

Thread a blunt-ended n with a length of A through sts on machine and take off.

· MAKING UP ·

Join the other shoulder seam. Sew collar side seam on WS with neat stitching (this side will show with collar roll-over). Set sleeves in flat, matching centre of CO edge of sleeve to shoulder seam, and between underarm markers on back and front pieces. Join side and sleeve seams.

Sew cotton tape, correct length of front width from top of sleeve to top of sleeve, along back neck.

Mark centre on front and back pieces. With RS tog, sew cable edge of welt to COn edge of front and back, with button bands on welt cable patt piece meeting and overlapping at garment front. Turn button bands to inside on foldline and hem down. Fold welt facing to inside and catch down along whole width of garment.

On cuff-end of sleeves, run a thread of yarn A through all sts. Mark centre cuff. With RS tog, pin centre cuff to sleeve seam, cuff button bands meeting and overlapping at marker on sleeve. Ease gathering section only to fit cuff, and sew. Fold button bands to inside on foldline and hem down. Turn cuff facing to inside and catch down.

Thread drawstring cord through top of welt, the ends meeting at centre back. Knot each end of drawstring, to prevent it running back. Thread 2nd drawstring cord through welt bottom, from centre front, round to centre front. Finish as before. Make 3 button loops on right welt button band. Sew on buttons to left welt button band to correspond to loops. Make 2 loops on cuffs, sew on buttons to correspond as for welt.

Make cross-st decoration on sleeves with leather thonging, and attach bead decoration on cuffs and garment front, as illustrated on design outline sketch (*Fig 4 on page 12*).

ACORN

· machine-knitted slipover ·

This garment is machine-knitted using an oak tree bark punchcard. The design is not worked out in detail, just described in general.

Fig 8 shows the ribbed collar, porcelain acorn buttons, distressed leather oak-leaf cut-outs, bark pattern, mohair stripes, and cable pattern at the bottom.

8 Acorn slipover

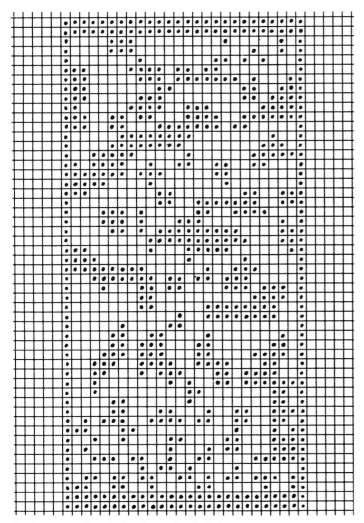

9 *Acorn punchcard of oak tree bark design*

look in burgundy for oak-leaf cut-outs (check washing instructions for leather).

An oak tree bark punchcard is shown in Fig 9.

An easy-to-knit cable patt is used on the welt of the design. Use 3 strands of the fine lambswool at approx T5.2*. K 4 rs. Cross st 1 in front of st 2 (i.e. lift st 1 onto a single transfer tool, move st 2 onto n 1, then place st 1 onto n 2). Bring crossed ns out to E position. These 4 rs from * form 1 patt. The n set-up is shown in Diag 1.

Here are some ideas for producing similar light weight machine-knitted fabrics combining interesting yarns.

Use a weaving patt, with fine mohair as the MY, and weave with a 3-ply wool.

Use high-sheen acrylics with mohair, and a long-float Fair Isle patt, and then cut the floats later (the reverse side of work will be the RS). Use a sl st patt, and alt with stripes of kid mohair and bouclé yarns.

This is a lightweight, short-sleeved style that could be worn either on its own, or over a shirt or polo-necked jumper. You could knit the pattern over the whole garment, but the patchwork effect is attractive, as it gives a contrast of texture and colours.

You can see in Fig 8 that different textures are combined. A mohair in brilliant sapphire blue is used on its own on the shoulders, and in stripes in the body.

If you do use a combination of yarns and textures, don't forget that you will have to knit a separate tension sample for each area. You may have to reduce or increase the number of stitches you have to get the right measurement, so you would take the work off the machine on waste knitting, and replace it onto the correct number of stitches.

Several strands of fine yarns used together produce a lovely soft, falling fabric that is suitable for blouses, soft dresses, full skirts, or anything that is gathered or loose-fitting. A design that uses wool, wool blends and cottons would be more suitable for thicker sweaters, jackets, straight skirts, suits, or more tailored dresses.

Use 3 strands of fine lambswool in browns and russets, with 2 strands of black lambswool for pattern. For stocking stitch use both 2 strands of fine superkid mohair, or 3 strands of heather-coloured lambswool. You will also need 4 acorn-design porcelain buttons, and distressed leather-

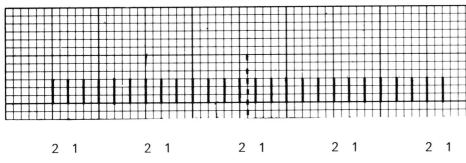

2 1   2 1   2 1   2 1   2 1

Diag 1 Needle set-up for cable pattern

The forsythia flowers early. It has beautiful yellow flowers that seem to dance in the wind.

The bluebells flower in the woods now, and there is a carpet of blue as you walk through the trees.

10 *Forsythia*

11 *Bluebells in the woods*

The bluebell flower is a lovely shape to transfer to a design.

It is the end of April and there is a mass of dandelions in the fields.

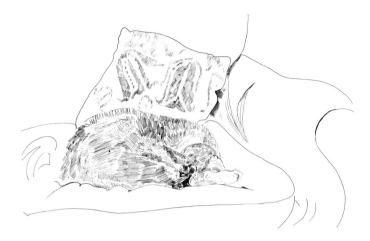

12a Bluebell cushion cover
12b Bluebell punchcard

13 Dandelions

*B*LUEBELL

· *machine-knitted cushion cover* ·

This cover is patterned on both sides, and then folded in half. The back and front pieces are knitted in one length (see *Fig 12*).

Knitted on a Passap Duomatic 80, using two colours and a self-punched card.

· SIZE ·

To fit a 40cm (15¾in) square cushion.

· MATERIALS ·

Yarns by Nina Miklin
150g (5½oz) Roma lambswool, white, shade 41 (3 strands used tog)
150g (5½oz) Milan superkid mohair, blue, shade 02 (2 strands used together)

· MACHINE ·

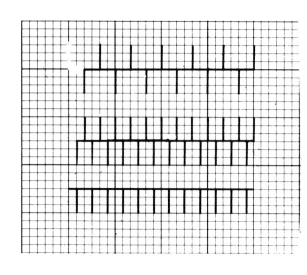

· TENSION ·

100 sts = 36.5cm (14¼in), 100 rs = 9cm (3½in) measured over patt.

· COVER ·

COn 110 sts on both beds. K in patt to RC888. CO.

· MAKING UP ·

Fold knitting in half, RS facing each other. Sew 3 sides of cushion, leaving a space so that you can remove the cushion filler and wash cover. Sew press fasteners to close this part of the seam.

Diag 2 Needle set-up for self-punched bluebell motif

Handle down
Orange strippers
T4.3/4.2
BX↔/BX←
Deco at 4
K 2 rs white
K 2 rs blue

KNITTING MOTIFS AND KNITTING FROM CHARTS

· INTRODUCTION ·

There are several charts given here for various animals. These needn't be just for a hand knitter, as they can be adapted as an intarsia chart (remember the animal will appear looking the opposite way to the picture), or as a chart for Swiss darning on the front of the jumper.

Read the notes on *Knitting from charts* and *Knitting motifs* below, and then look at the chart for the cockerel (*Fig 14*), the badger (*Fig 15*) and the shire horse (*see Fig 17*). There is a design given for a child's sweater using the shire horse chart.

14 Cockerel chart
Symbols on chart: dark brown (.) and light brown (blank)

First row

The badger would look best knitted in tones of grey – say dark grey and silver for the body, with the streak down his head in black.

You could knit the cockerel in many tones of reds, rusts and browns. In the chart it is suggested that he is knitted in light and dark brown.

· KNITTING MOTIFS ·

If you would like to knit in one of the motifs that are in the book, you will want it to be positioned in the centre of the garment front.

All the animal charts have approximately the same width, that is, they have the same number of stitches – 60 – but if you look at them, you can see that they are not all the same height, which means that they don't have the same number of rows.

The first thing to do is to find out the measurements of the front of the garment.

The smallest size of the shire horse sweater is: width 36cm (14¼in), length 33cm (13in), not including the neck measurement, as this is knitted after the motif is completed.

Knit a tension sample in the yarn. In our pattern, knitted in double knitting yarn on size 4mm (US6 ENG8) needles, we get 22 stitches and 28 rows to 10cm (4in).

Work out the number of stitches you must cast on, and the number of rows you must knit for the garment front, as follows.

width 36cm (14¼in) = 80 stitches
length 33cm (13in) = 92 rows
width of motif = 60 stitches, length of motif = 80 rows
   therefore:
80 (front stitches) minus 60 (motif stitches) = 20; divide by 2 for an equal margin on both sides = 10 stitches.
92 (front rows) minus 80 (motif rows) = 12; divide by 2 for equal margin at top and bottom of motif = 6 rows.

This has worked out a central position for the motif.

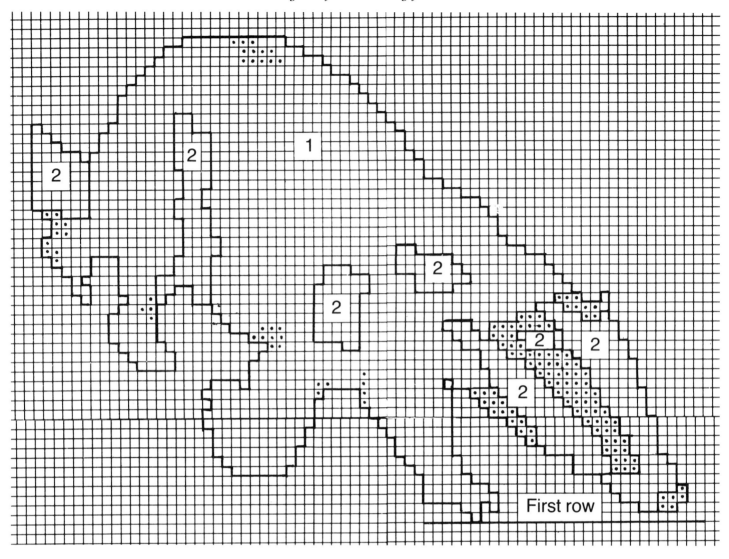

15 *Badger chart*
Symbols on chart: black (.) grey (1) and white (2)

· **K**NITTING FROM CHARTS ·

Any of the animal motifs will look good on the front of a sweater, but, as you can see from the charts, they are not all the same size (the shire horse, for instance, is taller than the badger). They are all approximately the same width, however; that is, they all have the same number of stitches within the motif.

Each square on the chart represents a stitch, and each line of squares, a row. The individual squares contain a symbol to indicate the colour to be used. It does take a lot of concentration to follow a chart, so it makes it much easier to have it enlarged on a photocopier; and then to fill in the squares with coloured pencils to match your yarn colours.

The charts are worked from the bottom upwards. The first row to be worked is marked '1st row'. In the shire

horse pattern the first two rows of the chart are written out in full. Read right-side rows from right to left and wrong-side rows from left to right. The charts are accompanied by a key showing the symbol that represents the yarn colour used in the pattern.

The shapes on your knitting won't look exactly the same as the chart, and the shire horse will appear slightly less elongated when it has been knitted. This is because the stitch is not exactly a square, but is actually more rectangular in shape.

The animal colourwork charts are worked in stocking stitch. As more than one colour is used, there are various different techniques to follow to deal with the extra yarns in each row.

When you come to the first line of the chart, make a knot with the new thread to the background thread and slip the knot near the margin. At the end of the work the two ends will be threaded through a few stitches, using a sewing needle, then cut off. To use a new thread in the middle of a row, use a sewing needle and thread it through the old

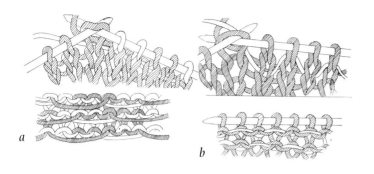

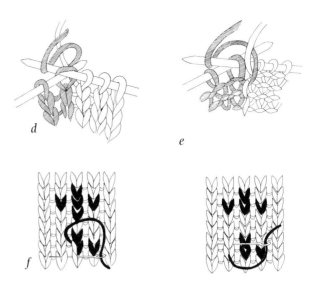

16 *Knitting from charts*
   a) *Stranding*
   b) *Weaving*
   c) *Bobbin shape*
   d) *Twisting yarns between colours*
   e) *Twisting yarns between colours on a purl row*
   f) *Swiss darning*

thread (at the end of work the two ends of 3 or 4cm [1½in] will be passed through a few stitches on the wrong side of the knitting, then cut off).

When the yarn not being used must be carried over a small number of stitches, you 'strand' the yarn, as follows. Work the given number of stitches in the first colour, then drop that yarn and pick up the second colour and work the given number in that. Drop the second colour and pick up the first colour, and carry it loosely across the back of the knitting to work the next stitch. Fig 16a shows RS (top) and WS (bottom) of work.

If the yarn not being used has to be carried over more than four or five stitches, you must weave it in behind the work with the other colour as it is knitted. Hold the yarn not in use in the left hand. On every second stitch take the yarn over the right-hand needle before drawing the loop through to make the stitch. Fig. 16b shows RS (top) and WS (bottom) of work.

When large blocks of colour are being worked, the yarns must be twisted together between each colour, rather than carried across the back. This prevents holes appearing where the colours meet, and also results in a fabric of single thickness. You can see how this is done from the sketch.

Each block of colour requires its own separate ball or bobbin of yarn. Using bobbins is a better method, as you can control the release of yarn from them, and keep the length of yarn you are knitting with short enough to prevent tangling. To make your own bobbin, cut out the shape from stiff cardboard (*Fig 16c*).

If you were following a more geometric pattern, with bold blocks of colour with the colours changing on diagonal or vertical straight lines, the yarns would need to be twisted at the back of the work on every other row only (*Fig 16d*). If the diagonal slants to the right, the yarns should be twisted on each knit row. On the purl row the crossing is not necessary as the yarns join automatically in the pattern (*Fig 16e*).

Swiss darning, or duplicate stitch, is an effective way of working different coloured patterns into ordinary knitting. It avoids having to work with lots of different yarns while you are knitting, and is perfect for adding small splashes of colour anywhere on your knitting.

· Swiss darning (*Fig 16f*) ·

Thread a large blunt-ended tapestry needle with yarn of the same ply as the background. Insert the needle from the back to the front of the work through the base of the first stitch. On the front of the knitting, thread the needle from right to left under the two vertical loops of the same stitch, but one row above. Pull the yarn through, and you will see that a stitch is formed. Don't pull the yarn too tightly – the tension of the new stitches should be the same as the background.

Re-insert the needle into the base of the stitch you are covering, and out to the front again through the base of the next stitch to the left. Pull the yarn through, and you have formed a Swiss-darned stitch.

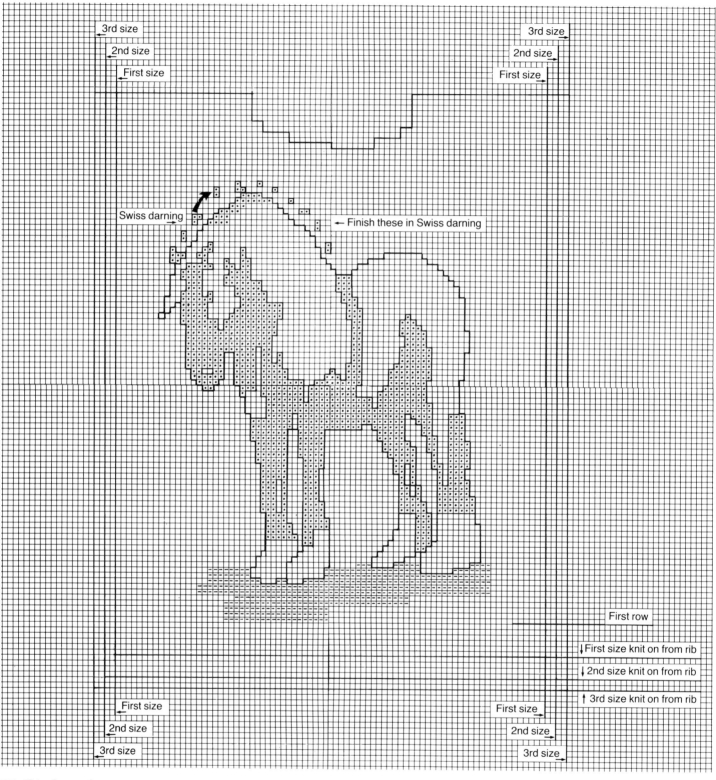

Swiss darning

← Finish these in Swiss darning

First row

↓ First size knit on from rib

↓ 2nd size knit on from rib

↑ 3rd size knit on from rib

17 *Shire horse chart*
 *Symbols on chart: A (blank outside motif), B (−), C (blank
 inside motif) and D (.)*

SHIRE HORSE

· child's design sweater ·

This neat and practical sweater is suitable for boys and girls. It is hand knitted in a machine-washable yarn that has the soft look of angora. There is very little shaping, and the sleeves and back are knitted plain in stocking stitch. There is a shire horse knitted in three contrast colours that covers the front of the jumper.

· MATERIALS ·

150(200, 200)g, 5½(7¼, 7¼)oz DK yarn by Texere, machine-washable koala angora-look, col A
50g (2oz) in each of 3 contrast cols (B, C and D)
1 pair each 3mm (US3 ENG11) and 4mm (US6 ENG8) needles
1 button

· SIZE ·

To fit age 4(6, 8) years.

18 Shire horse jumper measurements in three sizes

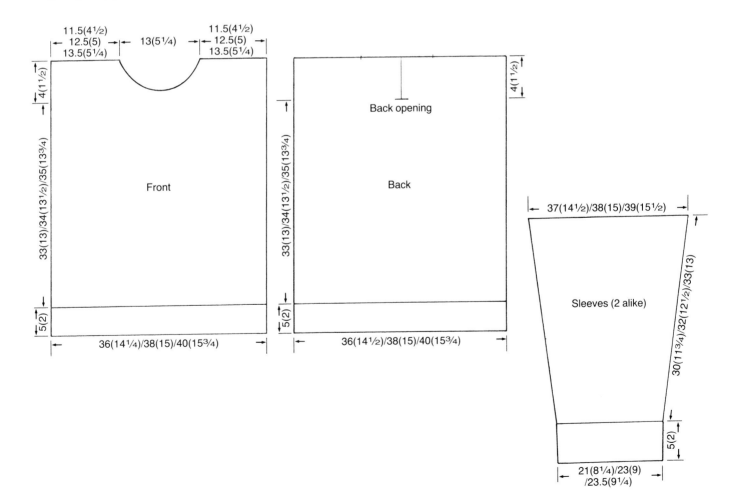

· TENSION ·

22 sts and 28 rs to 10cm (4in) over st st on 4mm (US5 ENG8) ns.

· FRONT ·

Using 3mm (US2 ENG11) ns and yarn A, COn over 80(84, 88) sts. Work 5cm (2in) K 1, P 1 rib (hereafter 1:1). Change to 4mm (US5 ENG8) ns and work 6(10, 12) rs in st st, beg with a K r.

Cont in st st, commence col patt from chart:
R 1, RS: K 40(42, 44)A, K 20B, K 20(22, 24)A.
R 2: P 20(22, 24)A, P 20B, P 40(42, 44)A.
These 2 rs establish position of chart.

Cont in patt on chart, keeping edge sts in A correct, until motif completed on r 84(88, 90). K 8 rs straight, 92(96, 98) rs, ending on a K r*.

· Divide for neck ·

Next r, P 40(42, 44) sts, turn, leaving rem sts on a spare n, and cont on these sts only for first side of neck. CO 8 sts at beg of next r and 5 sts at beg of foll alt r, and 2 sts at beg of foll alt r. Work 5 rs straight. CO rem 25(27, 29) sts.

Return to sts on spare n, and with WS facing, CO 8 sts, P to end. Complete 2nd side of neck to match first, reversing shapings. 102(106, 108) rs completed, counting from top of rib.

· BACK ·

Work in A only, as front, until *.

· Divide for back opening ·

Next r: P 40(42, 44), turn, leaving rem sts on a spare n; cont on these sts only for first side of opening.
Next r: K 1, P 1, K 1, P 1, K to end.
Next r: P to last 4 sts, K 1, P 1, K 1, P 1.
Keeping rib correct, work straight to r 102(106, 108). CO. With WS of work facing, rejoin yarn to sts on spare n, CO 1 st, P to end.
Next r: K to last 4 sts, P 1, K 1, P 1, K 1.
Next r: P 1, K 1, P 1, K 1, P to end.
Keeping rib as set, complete 2nd side of opening to match first side.

· SLEEVES (*2 alike*) ·

Using 3mm (US3 ENG11) ns and A, COn over 46(50, 52) sts. Work 5cm (2in) in 1:1 rib. Change to 4mm (US6 ENG8) and work in st st, inc 1 st at each end of ev 4th r until 82(84, 86) sts. Work straight until 84(90, 92) rs of st st have been completed. CO loosely.

· MAKING UP ·

Join shoulder seams.

· Neckband ·

Using 3mm (US2 ENG11) ns and yarn A, with RS of work facing, K up 60 sts around neck edge. Work 1cm ($\frac{1}{2}$in) 1:1 rib. CO loosely in rib.

Set sleeves in flat, matching centre of CO edge of sleeve to shoulder seam. Join side and sleeve seams. Sew a button at top of neck opening, work a button loop to match button on opp edge.

In May, the stream is a peaceful place to sit. The blackberry shoots dip in the water, and the sun casts a shadow through the old bridge (*Fig 19*).

19 Streamside in May

The shrub daphne is fully in flower now; its face could be either a square or a diamond shape (*Fig 20*).

The seeds of a sunflower are another diamond shape which is effective in a ridged knit on a jumper. You can see in Fig 21 how geometric shapes evolve from the sunflower (*a*), a dry stone wall (*b*), and trees (*c*). You could treat the landscape idea, behind the wall, as a patchwork in different stitches and patterns. For someone with a most basic machine that just knits stocking stitch, you could use the idea of the wall as a pattern for couching yarns (*Fig 21d*). If you used highly-textured yarns, it would be even more effective.

20 *Daphne in May*

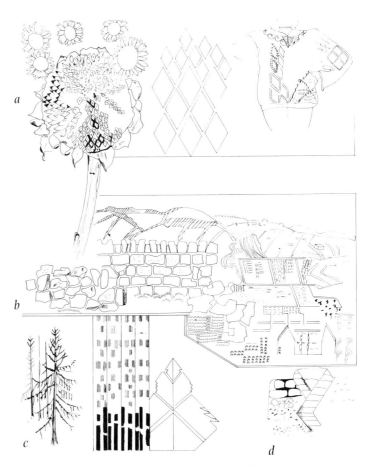

21 *Sketches from nature, reduced to a simple shape*

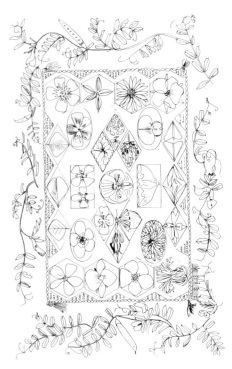

23 Meadow carpet reduced to a geometric outline

22 Meadow carpet

· Couching ·

Lay a thread along the line of the design and, with another thread, tie it down at even intervals with a small stitch into the fabric. The tying stitch could be a contrast colour to the laid thread.

Begin looking at flowers that could be geometric shapes (*Fig 22*). Some are obviously rounds and circles, and some stars and diamonds. The flowers in a meadow might look just a mass, but they can be seen as hexagons, pentagons, diamonds and squares. They would look lovely worked in embroidery on the knitted cushion cover (*Fig 23*).

Very often it is more effective in designing to contrast a swirling shape with a geometric one (*Fig 24*).

The fields are now full of the citrus yellow of the rape flower (*Fig 25*).

24 *Tulips in a vase*

25 *Rape fields in May*

26 Caterpillars

27 Wild honeysuckle

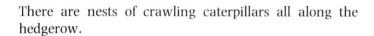

There are nests of crawling caterpillars all along the hedgerow.

The exotic scent of the wild honeysuckle lingers in the hedge.

A design for a machine-knitted cushion cover with a honeysuckle punchcard is given in detail in the next pattern.

HONEYSUCKLE

· machine-knitted cushion cover ·

28 Honeysuckle cushion cover

The cover is patterned on both sides, and then folded in half. It is knitted in a lovely jade green lambswool, but would look good if you used tones of colours such as russets and golds, or wine and pink.

· SIZE ·

To fit a 40cm (15¾in) square cushion.

· MATERIALS ·

Yarns by Nina Miklin
150g (5½oz) Roma lambswool, white, shade 41 (use 3 strands together)
150g (5½oz) Roma lambswool, jade, shade 45 (use 3 strands together)

· MACHINE ·

Knitted on a Passap Duomatic 80, using two colours and a self-punched card.

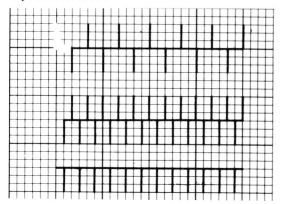

Diag 3 Needle set-up for self-punched honeysuckle motif

Handle down
Orange strippers
T4.3/4.2
BX↔/BX←
Deco at 4
2 rs white
2 rs jade

· TENSION ·

100 sts = 33cm (13in), 100 rs = 9.5cm (3¾in) measured over patt.

· COVER ·

COn 120 sts on both beds. K in patt to RC844. CO.

· MAKING UP ·

Fold knitting in half, RS facing each other. Sew 3 sides of the cushion, leaving a space so that you can remove the cushion filler and wash cover. Sew press fasteners to close this part of the seam.

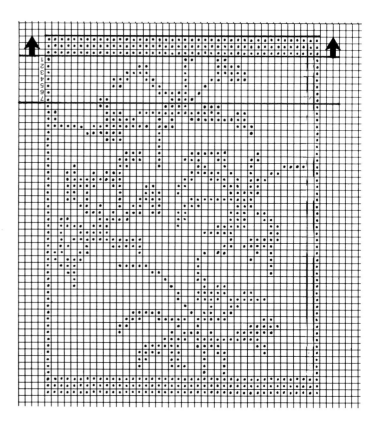

29 Honeysuckle punchcard

The buttercups are out now, and the field is a sea of gold in
the May sun.

30 Buttercups in May

The long grass almost hides the geese as they graze and snap at flies (*Fig 31*). A motif chart is given for the goose, and it is suggested you use grey and white for the background and contrast yarns (*Fig 32*).

31 Geese amongst the grass

First row

32 *Goose chart. Symbols on chart: grey (.) and pale grey or white (blank)*

Under the bank in the field there are several patches of
cowslips.

33 Cowslips

SHEPHERD'S PURSE

· machine-knitted cushion cover ·

34 Shepherd's purse cushion cover

The shepherd's purse is a pretty flower in the garden now. The front of this cushion cover has a pretty spriggy-looking allover pattern. The back is knitted plain in the background colour which is a lovely bright turquoise.

There are tassels at each corner, threaded through a dark green wooden bead, and these tassels are made on your knitting machine.

· SIZE ·

To fit a 40cm (15¾in) square cushion.

· MATERIALS ·

Yarns from Texere.
150g (5½oz) Spanish acrylic turquoise, shade 438, col A
25g (1oz) each apple green, shade 005, col B,
light green, shade 004, col C, and white, shade 000, col D.

· MACHINES ·

Suitable for a standard gauge punchcard machine. The cover was knitted on a Brother KH 830.

· PATTERN NOTES ·

Use T10, lower than for pattern, to knit stocking stitch on back. Although this yarn knits to approx double-knit patterns, it is soft, so the machine has no difficulty in knitting with it. It produces a lovely firm fabric which is ideal as a cushion cover.

The cover is knitted in one length of knitting. As you punch out the pattern, mark the colour changes, but bear in mind the number of rows that your particular machine 'swallows'.

· TENSION ·

26 sts and 34 rs to 10cm (4in) measured over patt (T10.1 approx).

· COVER ·

Using self-punched shepherd's purse PC. With col A, and T10.1, COn with a closed edge COn over 108 sts (54 either side of centre O). Insert PC in machine and lock on starter r. K to left. RC000. Set carr to patt Fair Isle. K to right.

Col B in feeder 2. Release PC. Change cols as folls (keeping col A in feeder 1 throughout; col changes refer just to col in feeder 2):
*K 12 rs with col B
K 21 rs with col C
K 12 rs with col D*
Rep from * to * twice more. RC136.
Mark both ends of this r. Remove PC. Set carr to K plain. T10. Col A in feeder 1. K straight in st st until RC272. CO.

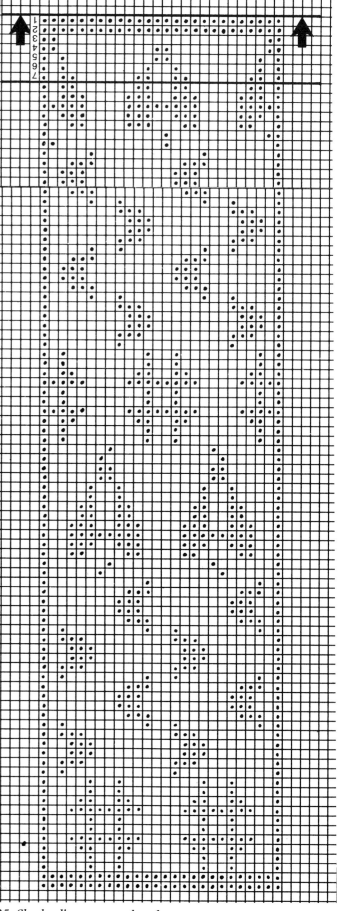

35 Shepherd's purse punchcard

40

41

· MAKING UP ·

Sew in all ends. Press with a warm iron, under a thick cloth.

Turn work so that RS are together, sew seams on 3 sides, leaving room on one seam so that you can remove filling when you wash cover. Sew in press fasteners to close seam.

Turn work so that RS are outside. Attach tassels to each of the 4 corners.

· TASSELS (4 alike) ·

Pull out needle 15 to full length on both sides of centre 0. Keeping a length of colour A in your left hand, wind with the right hand approx 16 times round the 2 needles. Cut the winding yarn, keeping a long length, then wind tightly round the centre of the loop, and pull through to make a knotting loop. Repeat the knotting loop. Remove from the needles. Fold in half.

Wind the long length round the top of all loops, approx 2cm (1in) down, then make another knotting loop, which you again repeat.

Thread the length of yarn through a needle, push through to the top of the tassel, then through a wooden bead; and with the right side of the cushion cover facing you, thread the needle through the corner point. Now bring it back out, again through the bead, and knot tightly. Cut. Now cut through all the loops at the bottom of the tassel.

· DESIGNING THE PUNCHCARD ·

The shepherd's purse is a small white flower of the wallflower family. It has a little heart-shaped fruit which looks like an old-fashioned purse when you hold it up to the light, for the seeds inside look just like money.

In Fig 36a the little flower is enlarged and then reduced to a geometric shape. The 4 petals now fit into the corners of a square.

The flower fits nicely into a square of 10 rows and 8 stitches (*Fig 36b*). A grid of 12 squares is drawn out (you can see it on the sketch outlined in a darker ink). The little crosses show how the geometric shape of the flower is drawn, enclosed in its square and how the shape is gradually built up. The shaded areas show how the outline reduces to a square, or, as it will be on the punchcard, a stitch. These will be punched out and knitted in the contrast colour as the machine knits a row, while the squares that are left blank will knit in the background colour.

Another grid of 12 squares is added to the original grid and you can see how the grid is extended for a 24-stitch pattern, that is, double the 12-stitch pattern.

The circles in the squares show how the flower shape is halved. In a repetitive pattern, the design will not fall just within the 24-stitch pattern outline, so you must design the card so that the pattern will follow on.

The two halves of the flower (shown on the grid within the broken lines) would appear together as one flower shape if this punchcard was knitted up.

The shepherd's purse punchcard has a 44-row repeat. In the last part of Fig 36b you can see how the pattern is halved, which is more attractive than having a row of flower heads, one below the other.

SUMMER

The wild chamomile, or scented mayweed, grows every-
where in the garden and amongst the stones on the path.

37 Wild chamomile

43

The orchid cactus suddenly flowers, with a bright pink
flower shaped like a flounced petticoat; but then it dies
down as quickly as it came (*Fig 38*).

38 *Orchid cactus*

39 *Flower blossom*
   a) dog rose b) rose c) rose d) blackberry e) musk rose

Now, in the middle of June, the flowers are all out beside the hedgerow (*Fig 39*). Many of these can be seen as a circle shape (*Fig 40*); even the delphinium, with a mass of petals to each flower, can be seen as a circle shape (*Fig 41*).

40 *Flowers in a circle shape*
  a) rosa b) pink c) marigold d) philadelphus e) geum
  f) honeysuckle g) double ranunculus h) single ranunculus
  i) pansy

41 *Delphinium*

The dog rose is one of the most beautifully delicate flowers in the hedge.

42 Dog rose

The sweet william flowers are seen as several shapes.

43 Sweet william flowers

Borage flowers are perfect to draw as they have so many shapes. The stem 'unhinges' from the flower, and is a perfect star.

44 Borage

Anemones have beautiful seed-heads, and delicately-pointed leaves.

45 Anemones

CIRCUS

· hand-knitted sweater ·

The inspiration for this circus sweater came from seeing the bobbing heads of begonia and fuchsia flowers as they were blown in the wind. They looked just like the folds and flounces of the dresses of dancers from a Toulouse-Lautrec painting.

· COLOURS ·

The colours are so strong in the sweater that they made me think of a circus, where there's constant movement and bright colours. Because the mood of the design needed to vibrate and dazzle, I used colours that would do just this. If you mix shades of one colour together, such as the pink and scarlet, and the jade and emerald, the effect is very strong.

· STYLE ·

This short cropped style isn't easy to wear if you have a large bust, as it rather chops the figure. You can get over this by wearing a longer-line jumper underneath and having a layered look. The under jumper should come at least 25cm (10in) below the line of the circus. Carry the black of the jumper down the whole figure if you are large on the hips.

The style is perfect for those with small busts and waists as it will round them out.

The wide collar means that this would be a perfect shape to knit up for winter, as you could wear a jumper underneath with a shawl or hooded collar, and complete this winter ensemble with jogging trousers, or high-waisted paratroopers'-style trousers.

· DESIGN ·

This hand-knitted loose-fitting sweater has exaggerated sleeves, a twisted rib, and an exciting border on the collar and round the bottom of the sleeves (*Fig 47a*). The design is knitted in stocking stitch and combines different textures and colours. The front has coloured motifs of circles and triangles that are decorated and transformed into a circus scene with a clown and dancing figure (*Fig 47b*).

· SIZE ·

A loose size to fit 81–91cm (32–36in) bust.

· MATERIALS ·

Yarns from Texere
200g (7¼oz) mohair, jade, col A
250g (9oz) mohair, black, col B
20g (1oz) pure angora, pink, shade 59, col C
100g (3¾oz) cotolux slub, green, shade 289, col D
250g (9oz) pure cotton, red, shade 273, col E
100g (3¾oz) *yarn is used double*, lurex, blue, shade L8, col F
1 pair each 4mm (US5 ENG8) and 5mm (US7 ENG6) needles
1 triangular red button

· FIBRE CONTENT ·

Brushed mohair – 75% mohair, 15% wool, 10% nylon
Cotolux slub – 64% cotton, 29% rayon, 7% nylon
Lurex – 65% viscose, 35% lurex

47b Circus motifs for front
Symbols on chart: A (.), B (blank), C (−), D (+) and
E (\)

46 Circus

47a Circus motifs for collar and cuffs
Symbols on chart: B (blank), D (+), E (\) and F (/)

· PATTERN NOTES ·

It is very difficult indeed to count rows on mohair, particularly black, so you will find that measurements of the work are given, rather than the number of rows.

· TENSION ·

16 sts and 18 rs to 10cm (4in) measured over st st on 5mm (US8 ENG5) ns.

· BACK ·

With 4mm ns and yarn E, COn 90 sts. Work rib as follows:
R 1, RS: sl 1 knitwise, * K 1 through back of loop, P 1 *, rep from * to * to last st, K 1.
R 2, WS: sl 1 knitwise, * K 1, P 1 through back of loop *, rep from * to * to last st, K 1.
Rep these 2 rs.
R 5: rep r 1.
R 6: K across all sts.
Rs 7–12: rep rs 1 and 2.

48 Circus measurements

Change to 5mm (US7 ENG6) ns and yarn B. Work in st st, beg with a K r, until work measures 42cm (16½in), measured from top of rib, ending with a WS r (76 rs).

· Divide for neck ·

Next r: K 28, turn, leaving rem sts on a spare n, and cont on these sts only for left side of neck. CO at neck as shown on chart for front (work from the instructions for the decs only, not the motifs). Cont straight in st st until 7cm (2¾in) are completed, measuring from sts CO for neck. CO rem 24 sts.

With RS facing, rejoin yarn to sts on spare n, take off 34 sts onto st holder, K to end of r. Complete the 2nd side of neck according to front neck chart.

· FRONT ·

COn and K rib as for back.

Change to 5mm (US7 ENG6) ns and commence patt from chart when you have completed the work in st st before the col motifs beg. Use separate balls of yarn for each col, and twist yarn between cols to avoid holes, as follows.
R 1 of col motif, RS: K 9B, K 1C, K 80B.
R 2 of col motif: P 79B, P 2C, P 9B.

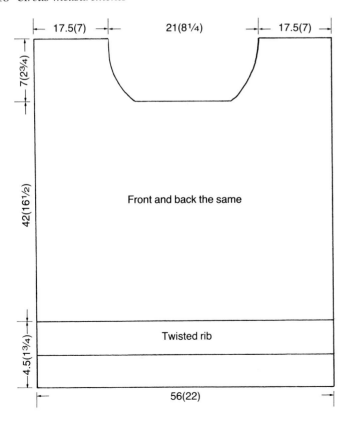

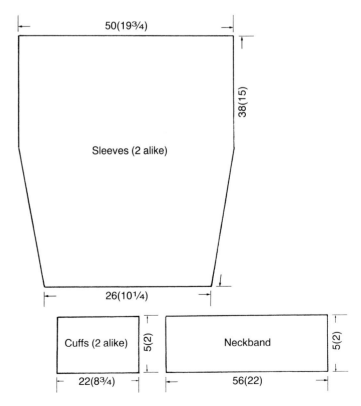

Work in patt until work measures 42cm (16½in), ending with a WS r (76 rs).

· Divide for neck ·

Dec work following instructions as for back neck, working patt motifs from chart at the same time.

· SLEEVES (*2 alike*) ·

With 5mm (US7 ENG6) ns and WY, COn 42 sts. K a few rs, then change to yarn A, and work in st st, inc 1 st at each end of the next and ev foll alt r until you have 80 sts. Cont straight until 38cm (15in), 68 rs have been worked. CO loosely.

· MAKING UP ·

· Cuff band (*2 alike*) ·

With RS of sleeve facing, and using 4mm (US5 ENG8) ns, pick up 42 sts from COn end, picking up from first r knitted in A. Work 10 rs of neck and cuff band patt motif from chart in patt cols, weaving in yarns behind work as you K.

In yarn C, P 1 r (foldline). Cont in C, work 4 rs in st st, beg with a P r. CO. Join right shoulder seam.

· Neckband ·

Using 4mm (US5 ENG8) ns, WS of front facing and yarn B, pick up and P 10 sts from side of front neck, 34 sts from st holder, then 10 sts from opp neck side. Rep for back piece (108 sts).

RS work facing, work 10 rs of neckband patt motif from chart in patt cols, weaving in yarns behind work as you K.

In yarn C, P 1 r (foldline). Cont in C, working 13 rs in st st, beg with a P r. Run a thread of col C through sts.

Turn neckband to inside and catch down sts. Join left shoulder seam.

Set sleeves in flat, matching the centre of the CO edge of sleeve to the shoulder seam. Join side and sleeve seams.

Sew a button on neckband opening. Make a loop on edge of corresponding opening.

Turn cuff facings to inside and catch down.

· Decorative detail on front ·

Study the design outline sketch. Cut out the leg shape in paper (shown in sketch), and use as a template to cut 2 legs in silk material.

St around the motif raw edges either by machine, using a close medium-width zig-zag st, or by hand, using a close blanket st; or allow a 5mm (2in) underlap when you cut out from the paper template, and then turn under and hem down. Overstitch in silk around leg shape.

Work a chain st outline around the diamond-shaped patt motifs for a clown shape, and around the 2 circles above the clown as a circus hat shape. Use a strand of the lurex for chain stitch decoration. Sew on sequins at random, if you wish.

· DECORATIVE EFFECTS ON THE · · BASIC DESIGN SHAPE ·

If you knit the basic garment shape and change the pattern content, there is a great deal of scope. The style demands some flamboyant decorative touches, and you can add fringing, braid, embroidery and large knitted strips in bright colours. Fig 49a shows a pleated soft collar, Pierrot-inspired cuffs, and flower decoration on the arm. There is also hand embroidery on the welt, and decorative buttons on the welt. Stem stitch (*Fig 49b*), satin stitch (*Fig 49c*) and hand-worked embroidery (*Fig 49d*) are used to great effect.

If you have a sewing machine, use a zig-zag stitch over several strands of a bright cotton yarn and attach to the garment with beads (*Fig 49e*). Use stem stitch for outlining hand-worked embroidery, and satin stitch and blanket stitch to create a raised effect on flower shapes.

Stem stitch is worked from left to right, taking regular, slightly slanting stitches along the line of the design. The thread always emerges on the left side of the previous stitch.

Satin stitch is a series of straight stitches worked closely together across a shape. You can work some chain stitching within the shape first to form a padding underneath, and then work the satin stitch over them for a lovely raised effect.

An easy-to-make fringe is just strands of yarn threaded through an edge in individual tufts and then knotted together. To hand knit a fringe, which is initially knitted and then unravelled, cast on a number of stitches to the depth you would like for the border, plus the length you want the loops to be for the fringe.

The fringe is knitted in garter stitch, which means that

every row is a knit row. For this description, let us assume that you cast on 9 stitches, which allows 4 stitches for the border and 5 stitches for the fringe loop. Knit in garter stitch until the border fits along the edge to be fringed. Cast off one less stitch than the total number of stitches you allowed for the border. Cut the yarn from your ball of wool and thread it through the last border stitch. You will have 5 stitches on the left-hand needle; now slip these off the needle.

Unravel the loops, beginning at the lower edge. You can pull gently at the stitches so they unravel. Don't worry that the 5 fringe stitches might unravel further, because they will not. When you have unravelled all along the line of ringing; sew the vertical garter stitch border at the top edge to the edge you want to cover with the fringe.

To sew the fringe to the border, turn it upside down so that the straight edge is level with the border, and then catch down with neat slip stitch along the straight edge. Fold the fringe over so that it hangs in the right direction. This vertical border hand-knitted fringe looks more attractive than the individual tufts that are threaded through the border and then knotted, as this can be too thick on a knitted edge.

Fig 49f shows a hand-knitted fringe on the sleeve; there is also a back panel of the checked pattern for interest.

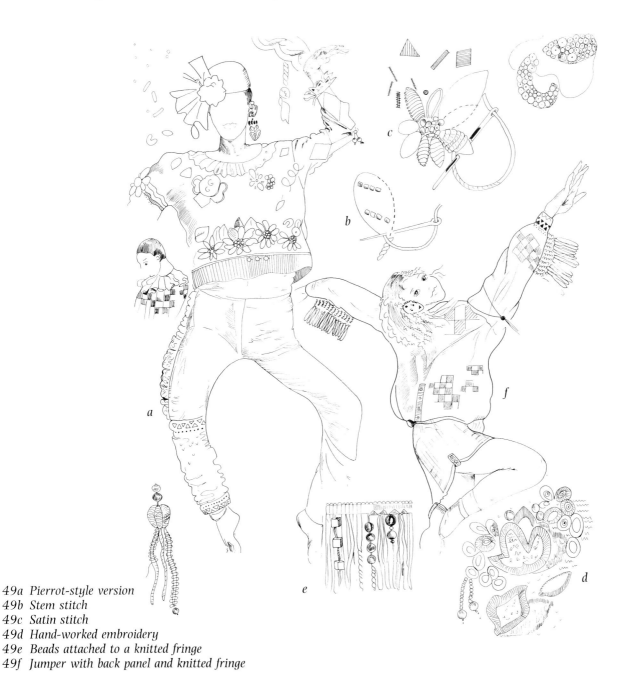

49a *Pierrot-style version*
49b *Stem stitch*
49c *Satin stitch*
49d *Hand-worked embroidery*
49e *Beads attached to a knitted fringe*
49f *Jumper with back panel and knitted fringe*

PATTERNS OF NATURE
· machine-knitted bedspread ·

Waves make patterns in the sand; you can see the punchcard that was inspired by the movement of the water (*Fig 52b*).

50 Patterns on the shore

If you punch out the various punchcards in a continuous pattern, allowing perhaps 20 rows of a plain background colour between each pattern, you can make a bedspread (*Fig 51*). Knit a lining in background, so that you can pad your bedspread for extra warmth.

51 Bedspread

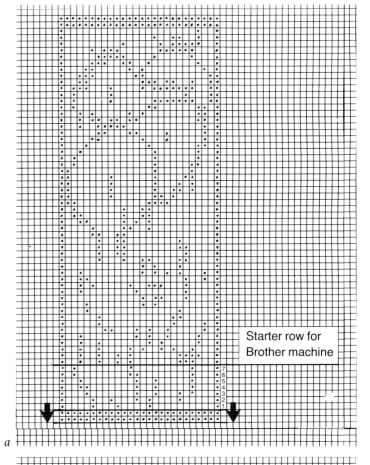

Starter row for Brother machine

a

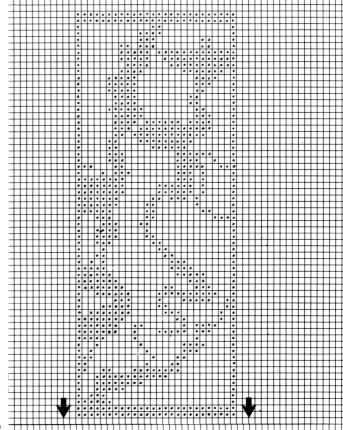

b

52 Bedspread punchcards a) Sheep b) Pattern on the shore c) Flowers and leaves d) Border tree pattern

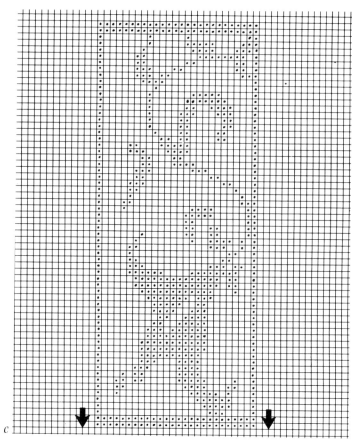

c

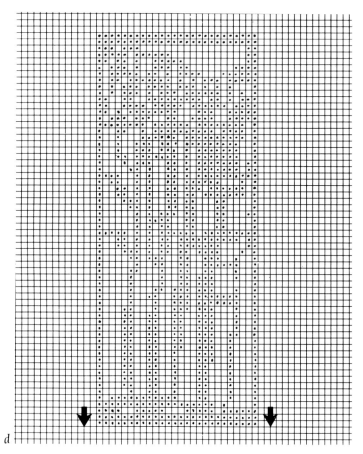

d

Cast on across the whole machine and knit to the length you require; you can sew these strips together to get the width you want (*Figs 52 and 53*).

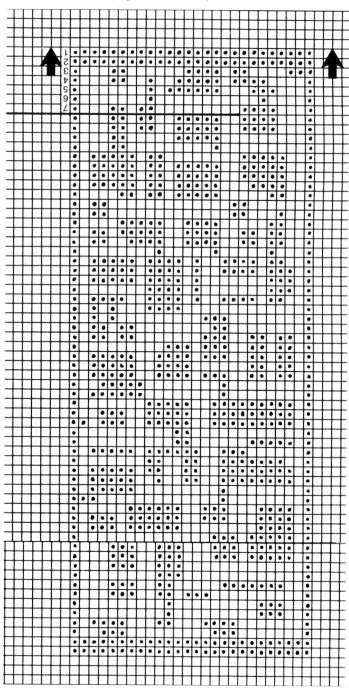

53 *Drystone wall punchcard*

There is plenty of colour from the flowers in the greenhouse in June.

54 *In the greenhouse*

55 *Elderflowers*

The elderberry bush is also out in bloom, with a mass of tiny white star-shaped flowers (*Fig* 55).

The orchard is full of the fragrance of apple blossom, and the cows lie contentedly in the long grass (*Fig* 56).

56 Blossom in the orchard

If it's a good year for apples, the cider will be extra strong.

57 Apple blossom and its fruits

LIGHTNING DESIGN

Sometimes in the summer there are storms too, as well as sunshine. I've given an impression in Fig 58 of low thundery clouds, and there's a streak of lightning that inspires the idea for this textural sweater. It is hand-knitted, and the blocks of different colours should look like mountains rising above a lake.

On the graph (*Fig 59*) you can see the suggested layout for the blocks. I would use a chunky-type yarn as the background, with a flecked rayon for the water, and a mohair for the mountain range.

When you are knitting a landscape of various textured yarns, you could use different tones of one colour. Tone is the variation between light and dark, and gives interest to an otherwise flat-looking surface. Dark colours give a richer effect, shiny ones reflect light, and raised stitches give a greater contrast in depth between light and dark. Dark colours also make lighter colours appear much brighter.

It would be fun to use a different type of bobble stitch for each block. You could use popcorn stitch for the mountain range, detached clusters in a shiny silk for the water, and trinity stitch for the block below the 'lake'.

· POPCORN STITCH ·

COn a multiple of 6 sts plus 5 extra.
R 1, WS: P to end.
R 2: K 2 (K 1, P 1, K 1, P 1, K 1) all into the next st; turn and K these 5 sts; turn and P 5. Using point of left-hand n, lift 2nd, 3rd, 4th and 5th sts over first st and off right-hand n (called make bobble or MB). * K 5, MB, rep from * to last 2 sts, K 2.
R 3: P to end.
R 4: * K 5, MB, rep from * to last 5 sts, K 5.
These 4 rs form the patt.

· DETACHED CLUSTERS ·

COn a multiple of 6 sts plus 5 extra.
R 1, WS: P to end.
R 2: K to end.
R 3: * P 5 (wool forward to make one st, K next st) 3 times into same st, so making 6 sts out of one. Turn and P these 6 sts. Turn and sl 1, K 5. Turn and sl 1, P 5. Turn and sl 1, K 5. Turn and (P2 tog) 3 times. Turn and sl 1, K 2 tog, pass sl st over (called make cluster, or MC). Rep from * to last 5 sts, P 5.
R 4: K to end.
R 5: P to end.
R 6: K to end.
R 7: P 2, * MC, P 5; rep from * to last 3 sts, MC, P 2.
R 8: K to end.
These 8 rs form the patt.

· TRINITY STITCH ·

COn a multiple of 4 sts.
R 1, WS: * (K 1, P 1, K 1) all into next st, P 3 tog; rep from * to end.
R 2: P to end.
R 3 * P 3 tog (K 1, P 1, K 1) all into the next st; rep from * to end.
R 4: as r 2.
These 4 rs form the patt.

58 *Lightning jumper*

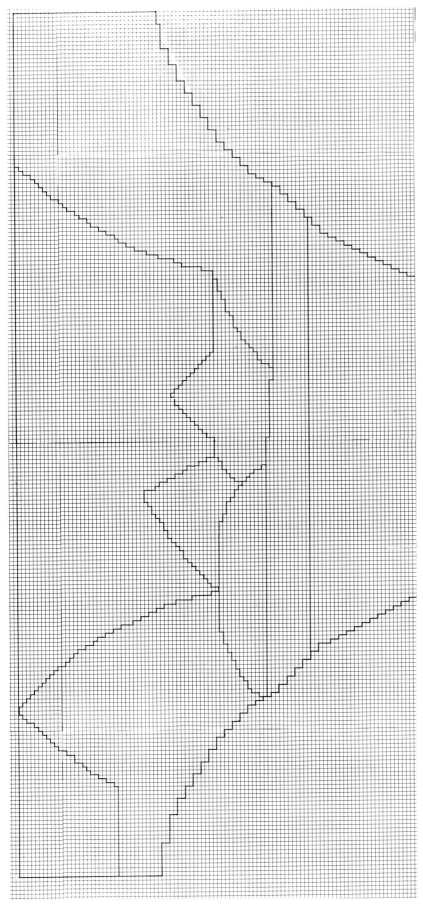

59 *Suggested graph layout to Lightning jumper for a one size pattern, approx. 81–96cm (32–38in).*

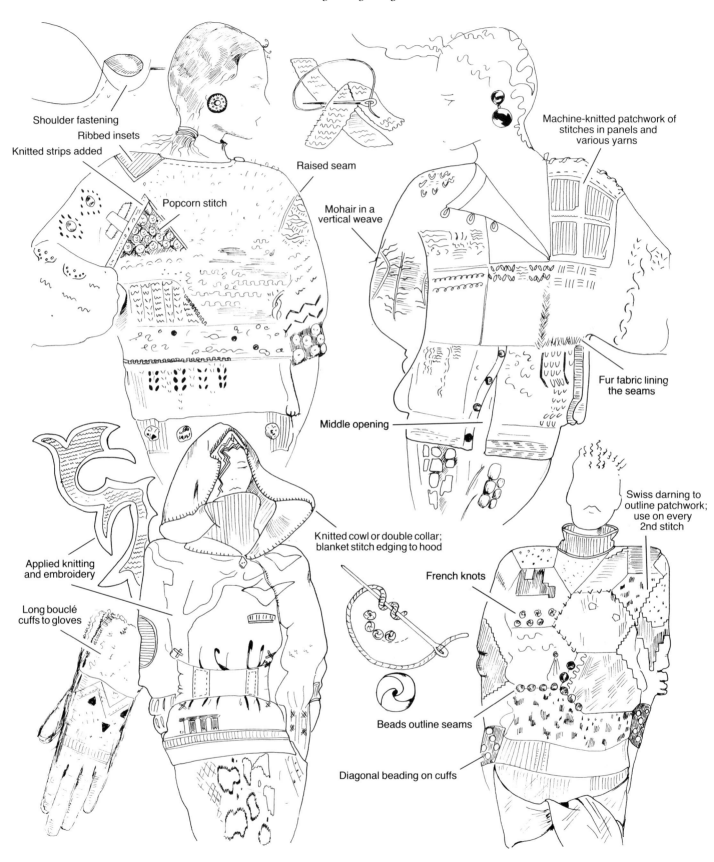

Shoulder fastening

Ribbed insets

Knitted strips added

Raised seam

Popcorn stitch

Mohair in a vertical weave

Machine-knitted patchwork of stitches in panels and various yarns

Fur fabric lining the seams

Middle opening

Applied knitting and embroidery

Long bouclé cuffs to gloves

Knitted cowl or double collar; blanket stitch edging to hood

Swiss darning to outline patchwork; use on every 2nd stitch

French knots

Beads outline seams

Diagonal beading on cuffs

60 Lightning – interpreted in various ways

A flower that introduces another shape is the scabis, sketched at the end of June. It has curled heads at the centre of the flower that form a mass of pentagon shapes.

61 Scabis

Hogweed has little black tips to each flower.

62 Hogweed

A stone wall provides the perfect background for a patchwork of flower shapes.

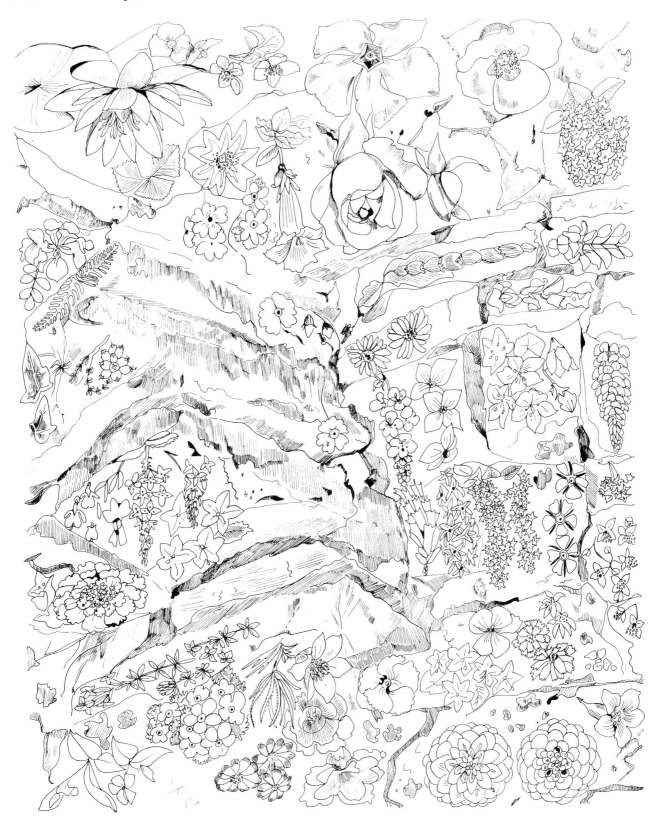

63 Wall flowers in the summer

DAFFODILS

· hand-knitted jumper ·

This textured, geometric design to a summer sweater uses a white background yarn that looks just like cotton.

· SIZES ·

To fit 81–86(91–96, 101–106, 111)cm, 32–34(36–38, 40–42, 44)in bust.

· MATERIALS ·

Yarns from Texere.
600 (600, 650, 700)g, $21\frac{1}{4}$ ($21\frac{1}{4}$, 23, $24\frac{3}{4}$ oz) 12-ply Spanish acrylic, white, shade 297, col. A.
25g (1oz) silk, red, shade 279, col B.
50g (2oz) silk, cream, shade 279, col C.
25g (1oz) slub, beige, shade 289, col D.
25g (1oz) cotton, yellow, shade 273, col E.
50g (2oz) slub, white, shade 289, col F.
50g (2oz) slub, red, shade 289, col G.
1 pair each 4mm (US5 ENG8) and 5mm (US8 ENG6) needles.

· PATTERN NOTES ·

Work pattern from chart. To avoid holes on work, take care to cross yarns on wrong side of work on each row at every colour change. The yarn from the last stitch must pass over the yarn to be used for the next stitch.

The straight-across style for the neck is finished in crab stitch, which gives a very attractive and extremely firm edging to the neck.

Crab stitch is a double crochet edging that is worked in reverse, that is, from left to right instead of right to left, and gives a textured, bound edge.

Start by working a row of double crochet along the side of the knitting to be edged. Don't cut off this yarn. Make one chain, then insert the crochet hook into the previous double crochet to the right. Take the yarn round the hook and draw a loop through, so that you have 2 loops on the hook. Take the yarn round the hook again and draw it through both loops on the hook. Work into each double crochet in this way.

· TENSION ·

17 sts and 24 rs to 10cm (4in) measured over st st on 5mm (US7 ENG6) ns.

· FRONT ·

Using 4mm (US5 ENG8) ns and yarn A, COn 82(86, 90, 94)sts. Work 8cm (3in) in 1:1 rib. Inc 12 sts evenly across last row, 94(98, 102, 106)sts. Change to 5mm (US7 ENG6) ns and work 20 rs in st st, beg with a K r.

Commence chart patt, work in st st throughout, as foll:
R 1, RS: K in G to end.
R 2: P in G to end.
R 3: K 59(61, 63, 65)G, K 6E, K 29(31, 33, 35)G.
R 4: P 24(26, 28, 30)G, P 14E, P 56(58, 60, 62)G.
Cont in motif using the other colours until it finishes on r 110.

K straight in st st and A for another 20(26, 30, 34) rs. 130(136, 140, 144) rs completed after rib.

· Casting off for neck ·

All sizes have the same neck width.
Next r: Take off 26(28, 30, 32) sts and put on spare n. CO next 42 sts and put rem 26(28, 30, 32) sts on spare n.

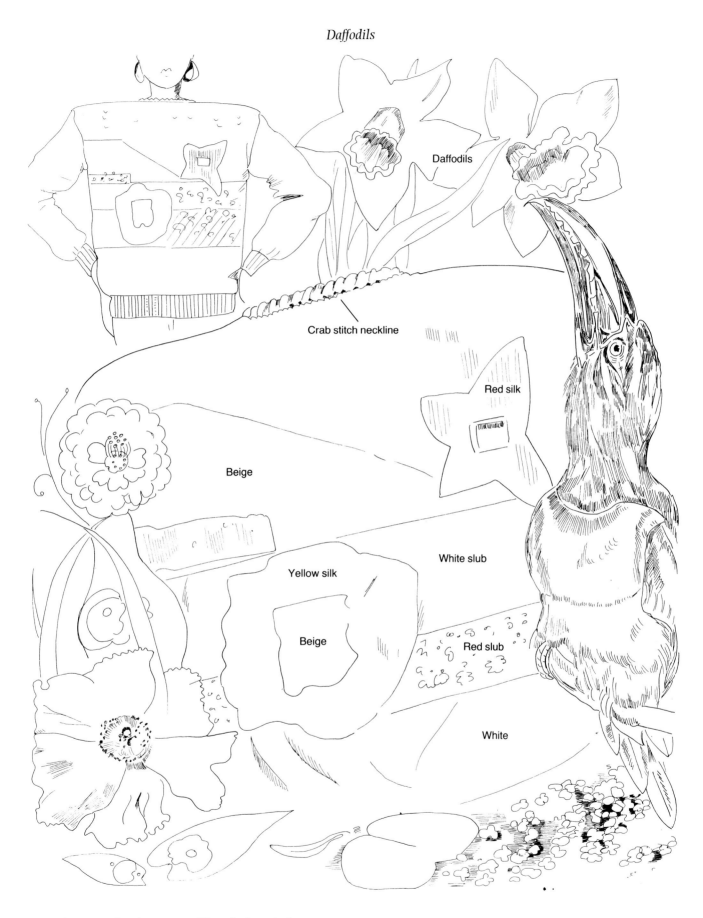

Daffodils

Crab stitch neckline

Red silk

Beige

White slub

Yellow silk

Beige

Red slub

White

64 *Daffodil design, with colours resembling the breast of a*
toucan, and the slub texture reminiscent of pond weed

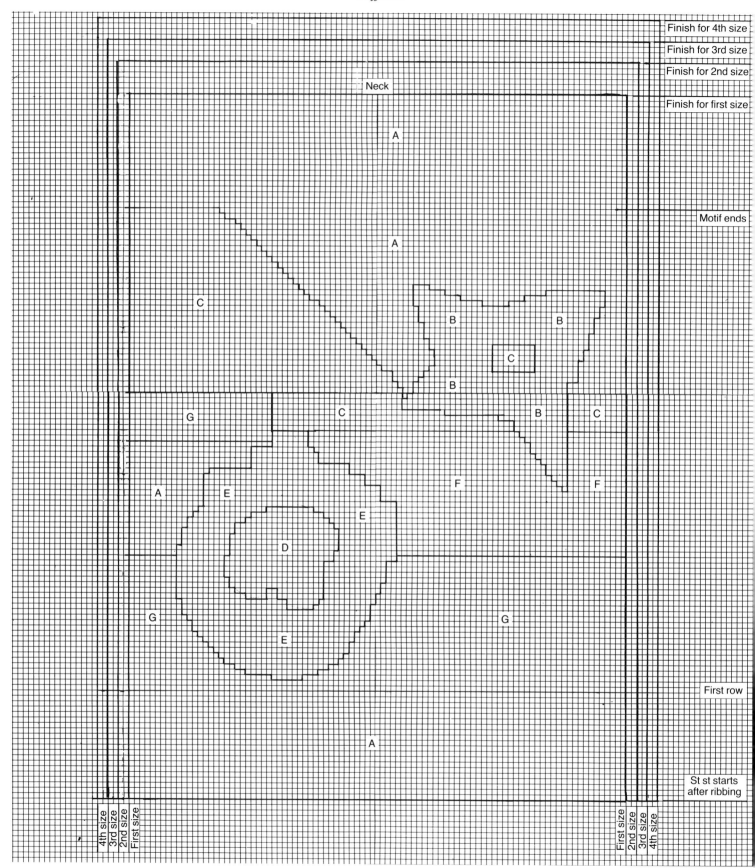

65 *Daffodil chart*

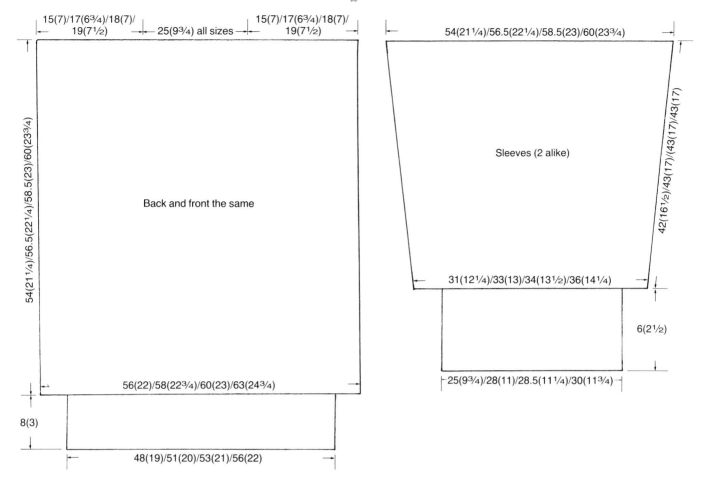

15(7)/17(6¾)/18(7)/ 19(7½)   25(9¾) all sizes   15(7)/17(6¾)/18(7)/ 19(7½)

54(21¼)/56.5(22¼)/58.5(23)/60(23¾)

54(21¼)/56.5(22¼)/58.5(23)/60(23¾)

Back and front the same

Sleeves (2 alike)

42(16½)/43(17)/(43(17)/43(17)

31(12¼)/33(13)/34(13½)/36(14¼)

6(2½)

56(22)/58(22¾)/60(23)/63(24¾)

25(9¾)/28(11)/28.5(11¼)/30(11¾)

8(3)

48(19)/51(20)/53(21)/56(22)

66 *Daffodil measurements*

· BACK ·

Work in A only. Knit ribbing and shaping as given for front. The back is knitted plain with no motifs.

· SLEEVES *(2 alike)* ·

Using 4mm (US5 ENG8) ns and A, cast on 42(46, 48, 50) sts. Work 6cm(2½in) in 1:1 rib, inc 10 sts evenly across last row. 52(56, 58, 60) sts. Change to 5mm (US7 ENG6) ns and work in st st, at the same time, inc 1 st at each end of ev foll 4th r until there are 92(96, 100, 104) sts.

Work straight until you have worked 100(104, 104, 104) rs of st st. CO loosely.

· MAKING UP ·

Knit shoulder seam sts tog (RS facing). Set in sleeves, matching centre of CO edge to shoulder seams. Join side and sleeve seams. Finish neck with crab st.

Using the same shape of the daffodil summer sweater, but changing the content, you could use it for a background for an intarsia design in pastel-coloured cottons. Any sort of cable pattern will look good on cotton, and you could shorten the sleeves and add cord around the neck for a type of mock-cable effect.

A machine-knitter could use a 2-colour skip stitch pattern, and add a ribbed inset on the shoulders.

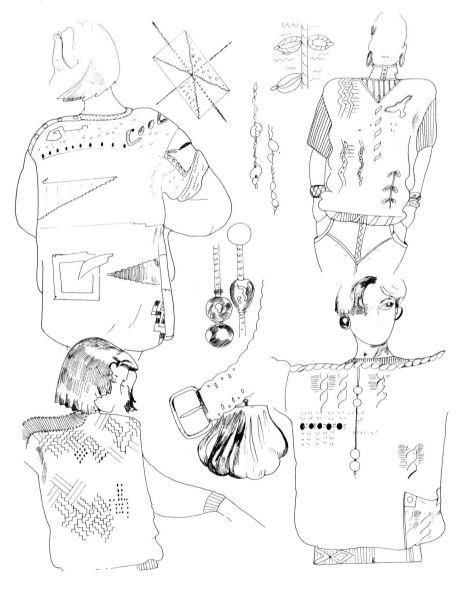

67 Ideas for summer sweaters

In July the meadows are a mass of wild flowers. You'll see hawkbit, vetches, mayweed, toadflax, ragwort, and trefoil.

68 Meadow in July

69 Just before harvest in the village

A busy time is coming in the countryside with the harvest. A farmer enjoys a moment of relaxation whilst the bees are humming in the lavender that surrounds the cottage door.

FOX

· hand-knitted sweater ·

This warm, yet light sweater with very little shaping is hand-knitted in a soft pure wool. A fox in a bright rust colour and beautifully toning shades strides across the front. The sleeves are knitted in the cream background colour, and the back and front finish at the neck in stripes of colour, mostly black.

There is also a pattern for leggings, to use up the wool left over from knitting the sweater.

· SIZES ·

To fit 86(91)cm, 34(36)in bust.

· MATERIALS ·

Yarn from Texere; all colours are Peruvian highland wool.
550g (19½oz) ref 4217, col A.
50g (2oz) of each of foll: black, ref 182, col B; dark rust, ref 5634, col C; light rust, ref 595, col D; pink, ref 5633, col E, and royal blue, ref 401, col F.
1 pair each 4mm (US5 ENG8) and 5mm (US8 ENG6) needles.

· PATTERN NOTES ·

The fox motif is worked from the chart in stocking stitch, beginning with a knit row. Join in and break off colours as required. Use separate lengths of yarn for each change of colour, linking one colour to the next by twisting them round each other on the wrong side to avoid gaps.

· TENSION ·

19 sts and 26 rs to 10cm (4in) over st st on 5mm (US7 ENG6) ns.

· FRONT ·

Using 4mm (US5 ENG8) ns and A, COn 84(94) sts. Work 5cm (2in) in 1:1 rib.

Change to 5mm (US7 ENG6) ns and work 20(36) rs in st st, beg with a K r.

Cont in st st, working from fox motif chart as follows:
R 1, RS: K 12(17)A, K 2B, K 23A, K 2B, K 1A, K 2B, K 42(47)A.
R 2: P 33(38)A, P 1B, P 8A, P 5B, P 23A, P 2B, P 12(17)A.
Cont until end of motif, ending on a K r. Work in st st and A until 110(126) rs have been worked, counting from top of rib, ending with a P r. Working in st st, K 2 rs E, K 4 rs B, K 2 rs F, K 6 rs B.

· NECK FACING ·

Sl 24(27) sts on each shoulder onto spare ns and cont in st st on centre 36(40) sts on 4mm (US5 ENG8) ns and B. K 6 rs for facing, inc 1 st at each end of ev alt r. CO loosely.

· BACK ·

K as for front, but omit fox motif.

70 Foxglove

First size

2nd size

First row

71 *Fox motif*
  Symbols on chart: A (blank), B (.), C (/), D (−) and
  E (+)

· SLEEVES (*2 alike*) ·

Using 4mm (US6 ENG8) ns and A, COn 46(48) sts. Work 5cm (2in) in 1:1 rib.

Change to 5mm (US8 ENG6) ns and work in st st, beg with a K r, inc 1 st at each end of the next and ev foll 5th r, until there are 80(84) sts. Cont without shaping until 102 rs have been worked, counting from above rib. CO.

· MAKING UP ·

Join shoulder seams. Sew side of neck facings, fold to inside (WS) of work and hem down.

Set sleeves in flat, matching centre of CO edge of sleeve to shoulder seam. Sew side and sleeve seams.

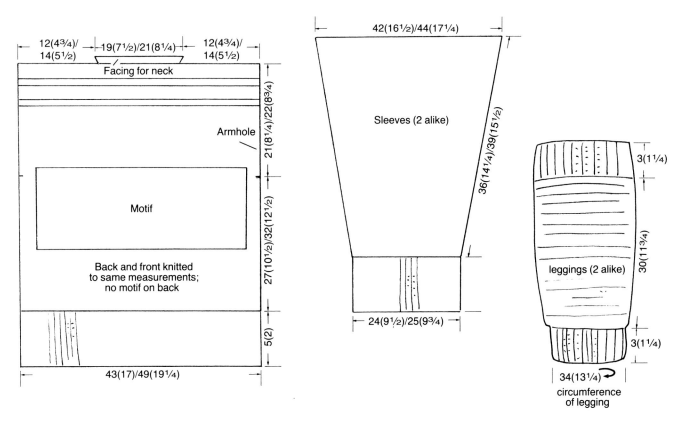

72 Fox measurements

LEGGINGS

The leggings are striped in the colours from the fox motif sweater. They weigh 225g (8¼oz), and you should be able to knit them from wool left over from the fox motif sweater. If you are short of one of the colours suggested in the pattern, substitute one of the other colours; but match the change in both leggings.

· TENSION ·

Yarn used double. 14 sts and 20 rs to 10cm (4in) measured over st st on 6½mm (US10 ENg3) ns.

· LEGGINGS (*2 alike*) ·

Beginning at top, with yarn D, and 6½mm (US10 ENG 3) ns, COn 48 sts and work in 1:1 ribbing for 3cm (1¼in). Cont in st st and patt: * 2 rs A, 2 rs F, 2 rs A, 2 rs C, 2 rs E, 4 rs D, 2 rs E, 4 rs C *. Rep from * to * 2 more times (60 rs), approx 30cm (11¾in).

In F, work 3cm (1¼in) in 1:1 ribbing. CO in ribbing.

· MAKING UP ·

Steam press, weave in yarn ends. Sew back seam with whip st (over-and-over st) on WS. Draw a few elastic threads through top ribbing.

SILVER ROSE AND LILY
· machine-knitted evening top ·

· LILY DESIGN ·

The gentle, flowing shape of a lily suggests elegance and calm, which is just what is wanted for an evening design; another design line that symbolises tranquillity is a ripple, or any undulating line. Having seen the effect of the lily shape, I could see it would look just right for the neckline of the top, particularly if it was outlined in pearls.

73 Lilies

74 *Silver rose – working out the desired style*

75 *Silver rose – various ideas for a rose motif*
  a) embroidered rose b) paperweight c) rose in lace
  d) rose picked out in machine weave knitting e) leather belt
  f) intarsia rose g) art nouveau-style rose
  h) damask rose

· ROSE DESIGN ·

The rose inspires so many different ideas as an outline, and it is a good exercise to sketch all the shapes you can think of (*Fig 75*), and then choose the one you think would be most suitable for a punchcard motif.

Having made your choice, you now have to produce the rose motif as a repetitive pattern on a punchcard (*Fig 76*).

If you look at a rose you see a circle shape. But for the punchcard it would be easier if it were a square or a diamond. The diamond shape, which is really a sideways or elongated square, seems perfect, as the first sketch I drew of the roses had them falling down a wooden diamond-shaped trellis (*Fig 76a*).

A diamond shape is another way of seeing two triangles. To see this for yourself, draw out a square on lined paper, measuring vertical lines at right-angles to the already drawn-in horizontal lines on the paper. If you make your lines the same length, you'll have a square.

You can see from Fig 76b that when you cross the square by a diagonal line (shown by a broken line in the sketch), you get two triangles; and if a diagonal is also drawn in the other direction, several different shapes, all based on the triangular outline, all emerge from it. You can also produce a hexagon or a star, and many more familiar geometric outlines.

When you are working out a pattern to put on a punchcard, you can use squared paper, but it's important to know that a knitted square needs more rows than the number of stitches to be a perfect square. An average knitted square is approximately six stitches and eight rows, though the proportions will vary with the type of yarn you're using.

The squared grids in Fig 76c show this simply. The smaller grid is an actual square; the longer one shows the extra rows you will actually have to knit to produce the same length as the first. That is, if you knitted up the number of rows of the second grid, it would come out the same shape as the first. So you can see that if you design straight onto squared paper, the motif will look shortened on the actual knitting. You can buy graph paper especially for the purpose that is slightly flattened, or you could use ordinary graph paper, and draw your motifs longer.

Fig 76d shows the shaded rose and leaf at the first stage, before they have been reduced to a geometric outline. Below that is how it looks when the outlines are drawn on the flattened graph paper, and you can see how elongated they look.

In the last sketch, a geometric shape is produced. The rose motif is crossed diagonally. The points of these lines are joined up (shown in the sketch by broken lines), and you can see how a sideways-shaped square or a diamond shape is produced.

· PRODUCING THE PATTERN ON · · THE PUNCHCARD ·

The rose motif was designed for a Passap Duomatic machine, which means that the punchcard has 40 stitches and 48 rows on the blank card.

To make this more simple, I visualised 20 stitches with a 24 row repeat pattern, which I further reduced to 10 stitches and 12 rows; this is, in fact, an ideal knitted square, with more rows than stitches.

The whole point of using a pattern on a punchcard is that it repeats one motif after another, which it must do in a simple and attractive way.

In Fig 76e a grid is drawn out representing a blank punchcard (i.e. containing 40 stitches and 48 rows). These are divided into four squares of 10 stitches and 12 rows each, so there are four complete squares on the punchcard. (The squares are drawn out in broken lines on the grid.)

For the design I had reduced the rose to a geometric outline in a diamond shape, so now I wanted to draw diamond shapes on the grid. As we have just seen, a square lattice crossed by diagonal lines gives a triangle, and hence a diamond. On the grid I drew a diagonal line from one side of a square to the other, and then repeated this on the three other squares surrounding it.

· THE GARMENT ·

This soft, lightweight evening top has a cobweb effect knitted in fine superkid mohair and lambswool. The yoke is knitted in silver-grey, while the sleeves and ribbed welt are in white. The remainder of the body on both back and front pieces uses a self-punched rose motif knitted in white mohair with a contrast of very fine grey lambswool.

The long ribbed welt is close-fitting to the hips, and pulls in the gently bloused effect of the body. The full sleeves are gathered at the wrist, and the cuff has a shell edging and is decorated with pearls and sequins. The back is divided to the bottom of the yoke, and fastens at the back of the neck with a pearl button. The V-neck shape on the front is filled in with a see-through material and outlined in a lily shape with a pearl trim.

Details of Silver Birch and Loose-fitting and Long machine-knitted jumpers

Badger motif knitted from a chart

Circus hand-knitted sweater

Daffodils hand-knitted jumper

Silver Rose and Lily machine-knitted evening top

Summer Country Flower hand-knitted jacket

Knot Garden machine-knitted bag

Flight Pattern hand-knitted sweater

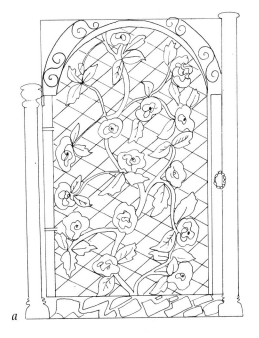

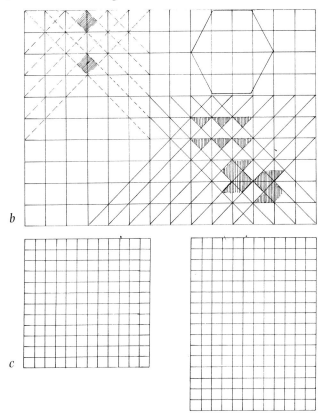

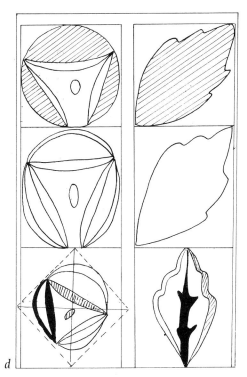

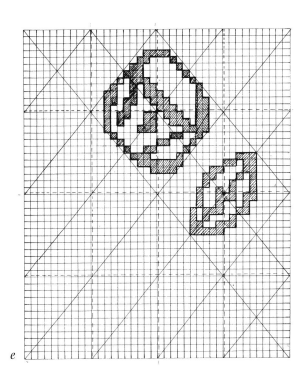

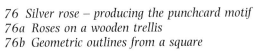

76 Silver rose – producing the punchcard motif
76a Roses on a wooden trellis
76b Geometric outlines from a square

76c Squared grids
76d The rose and leaf become a geometric design
76e Rose within a diamond shape

77 Silver rose and lily design

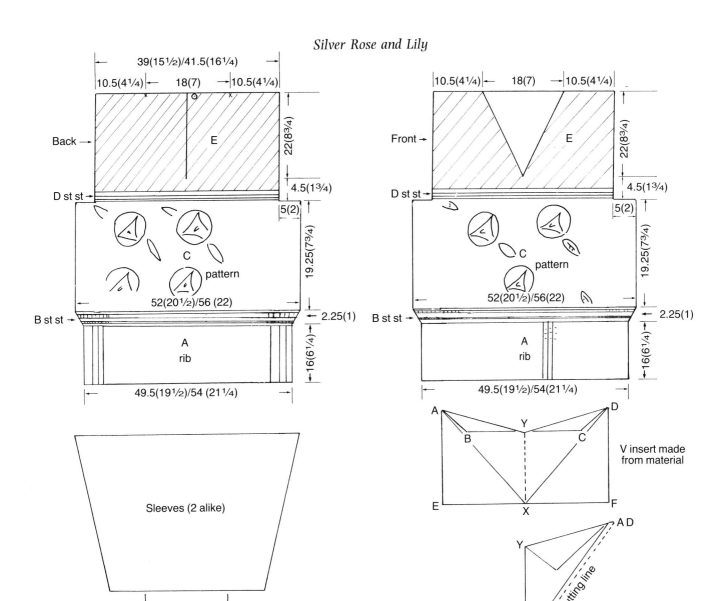

78 Silver rose measurements; shaded areas represent work in silver grey mohair

· SIZES ·

To fit 81–86(91)cm, 32–34(36)in bust.

· MATERIALS ·

Yarns by Nina Miklin. One strand of each used.
150g (5½oz) Milan superkid mohair, white, col A.
150g (5½oz) Milan superkid mohair, silver-grey, col B.
50g (2oz) Roma pure lambswool, grey, shade 29, col C.
Pearl button
Pearls, sequins, diamanté and pearl trimming
Shoulder pads
Water-erasable pen
24cm (9½in) square muslin
Fine elastic

· STITCH SIZE ·

Single-bed Fair Isle pattern 6/6. 1:1 ribbing, T3¾/3¾. Stocking stitch approx 6.

· PATTERN NOTES ·

This is knitted on a Passap Duomatic 80. Punch out the rose motif punchcard before starting; the needle set-up is detailed in Diag 4. Diags 5–7 show further needle set-ups.

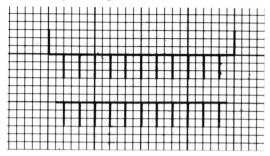

Diag 4 Needle set-up for self-punched rose motif

Handle down
Black strippers
T6/6
N/BX←
Deco at 4
2 rs A
2 rs C

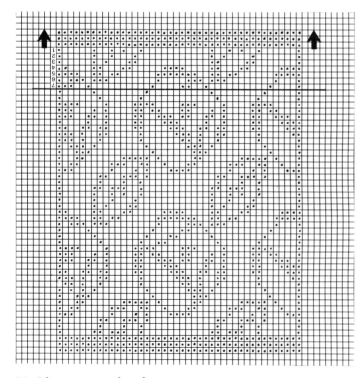

79 *Silver rose punchcard*

The design uses a combination of ribbing, stocking stitch, and single-bed Fair Isle, worked on the front bed of the machine. When dividing work for back opening, remember to bring row counter to right of work, and hang weights under division of work.

· TENSION ·

100 sts = 34cm (13¼in), 100 rs = 12cm (4¾in) measured over single-bed Fair Isle patt. 28 sts and 42 rs to 10cm (4in) measured over st st.

· BACK ·

* Tubular COn, n set-up as detailed in Diag 5, with yarn A over 138 (150) ns. T3¾/3¾, K in rib for 85 rs. (Lock at left) K 1 r T5/5. Bring intervening ns to WP on front bed. Transfer all sts to front bed, 138 (150) sts. RC86.

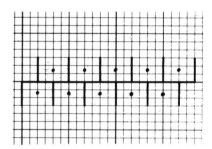

Diag 5 Needle set-up for double-bed 1:1 rib

Handle up
Orange strippers
N/N k on ev alt n on both beds

T6. Black strippers. GX/N. K 2 rs in A, 2 rs in B, *twice*, inc 1 st at both ends on next, then alt rs. 146/158 sts. RC94.
RC000. With A as main col, C as trimming col, insert patt as Diag 1, and set Deco. K in patt to RC181 (Lock on left). GX/N. Release Deco. T6. CO 18(21) sts at beg of next 2 rs. 110(116) sts remain. Carr on right.
RC000. K in st st alt rs of A and B, beg with 2 rs of B, to RC12. K in B to RC20(20)*.
Thread a separate ball of B through a 2nd feeding eyelet.

· Divide for back opening ·

RC000. Lock BX←. Put pushers for ns right of centre into rest position. Put pushers for ns left of centre into WP. Left feeding eyelet in Lock, K 2 rs (2 rs of the right half are being knitted). Change feeding eyelet, K 2 rs. Cont thus to RC184. Release both pieces on WK.

· FRONT ·

Knit as for back from * to *.

· Divide for front V ·

GX/BX. Put pushers under ns in work right of centre, and pushers under ns left of centre in rest position. T6, RC000. With yarn B, dec 1 st on next and then every 3rd r at neck edge (put pusher in rest position on each dec), until 29 sts rem. K straight to RC92. Release on a few rs of WK. RC000.

· Left side ·

As for right side, reversing shapings. RC92, release on WK.

· SLEEVES *(knit 2 alike, all sizes the same)* ·

Push up 74 ns on both beds. RC000. COn shell edging as Diag 6, and complete. (10 rs worked.) Transfer sts to front bed, 74 sts.

RC000. GX/N. Black strippers. Yarn A and T6, K in st st to RC64. Take off on WK.

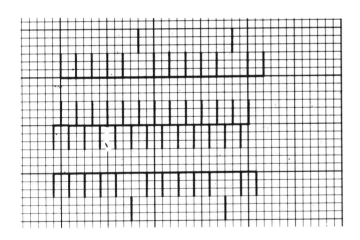

Diag 6 Needle set-up for shell edging on cuffs

Handle down
Orange strippers
T5/5
1 r N/N A
1 complete turn to left of handle
1 r N/N A
6 rs BX/BX B
2 rs N/N B

With WY, cast on 148 sts on the front bed, using the single-bed COn method shown in Diag 7. RC000. Change to yarn A, T6, K in st st, inc 1 st at each end of rs 14, 28, 42, 56, 70, 84, 98, 112, 126, 140, 154 and 168 (172 sts). K straight to RC182. CO loosely.

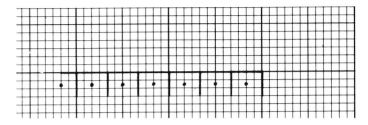

Diag 7 Needle set-up for single-bed COn

Black strippers
Alt ns up on front bed
GX/N, 1 r T2
Bring up all ns
GX/N, 1 r T5 on all ns
Cont in T6

· To join cuff to sleeve ·

Pick up sts from last r of MY before WK on cuff top and sleeve bottom, then, with RS facing each other, CO 1 st from cuff top (74 sts) to ev 2 sts from sleeve bottom (148 sts).

· MAKING UP ·

Join shoulder seams. Set sleeves in flat, pleating sleeve head to fit, matching the centre of the pleating on the CO edge of the sleeve to shoulder seam, and joining last few rs of sleeve to CO sts at underarm. Join side and sleeve seams to end of cuff. On WS of work, turn in small edging on back neck, and round to bottom of back opening on both sides. Sl st down. In yarn B, make 1 button loop at top of back opening, sew on button on opp opening to correspond.

Decorate cuffs to your choice in pearls and pearl-coloured sequins. Thread fine elastic along joining seam on WS of sleeve to fit your wrist comfortably.

· To decorate yoke ·

Lay work flat. Lay rose motif PC on top of knitting to one side of V neck. With a water-erasable pen, mark through the punched holes onto the knitting, marking out as much of the design as you want. Sew pearls over these marks; the motifs now have a raised outline of pearls.

· To make V insert for front ·

Fold measured muslin square ADFE in half (*see Fig 78*): A to D, E to F. At A–D end of fold, measure down 6cm (2½in) and mark. Cut to mark (Y). Fold back cut edges to opened square, and sl st down along lines YB, BA, YC and CD.

Again, fold in half, A to D, E to F. Middle line of square is YX. Either draw a line diagonally from X to A, and then from X to D, with a water-erasable pen, or sew with a tacking line. Measure a seam allowance away from this line and then cut.

Open out V insertion, pin close to the drawn line, then tack to WS of garment front, taking care that V is aligned to drawn-in line on material insertion. Turn in tiny hem of muslin and hem stitch down to WS of knitting. Pin, then sew pearl trim on RS of material insertion, along lines AX, XD, DC, CY, YB, BA, AY, and YD.

Cover shoulder seam, along to back opening on both sides, with diamanté trim. Thread fine elastic on WS of back and front pieces along welt seam line to gather slightly to your waist. As an optional extra, cover shoulder pads with grey lining material, then stitch in place.

Fig 80 shows (from top) the rose motif, an appliqué lily, and an intarsia design for a summer top.

80 *Silver rose – more patterns*

By harvest time the verges in the lanes and surrounding
the corn fields are a mass of poppies and grasses.

81 Meadow at harvest time

The poppy is a lovely shape, and it is easy to be inspired by it
(*Figs 82–84*).

82 *Poppies and grasses*

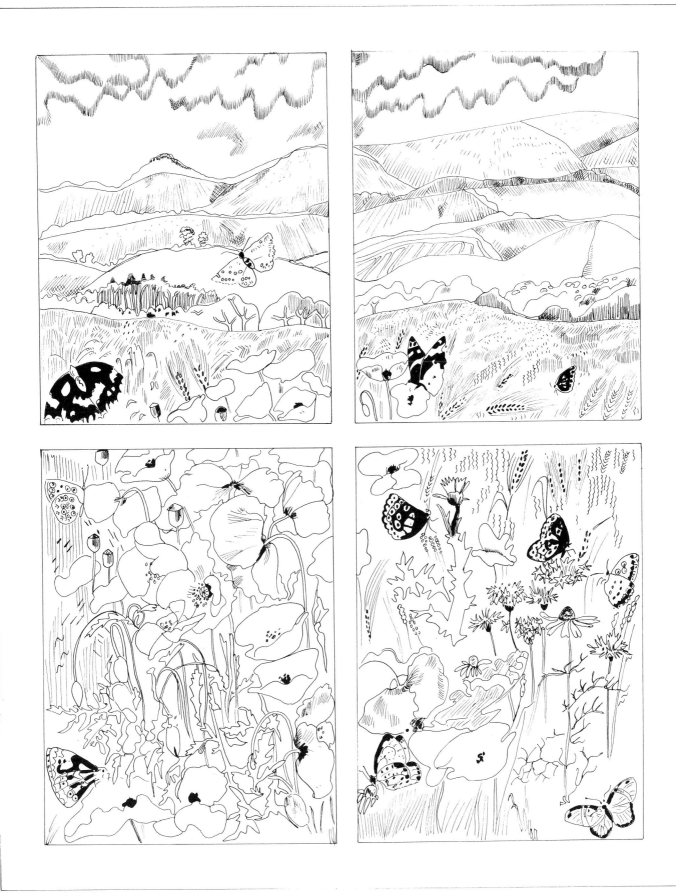

83 View out of the window

84a Poppies and landscape in their natural state . . .   *84b . . . and as reduced to a geometric outline*

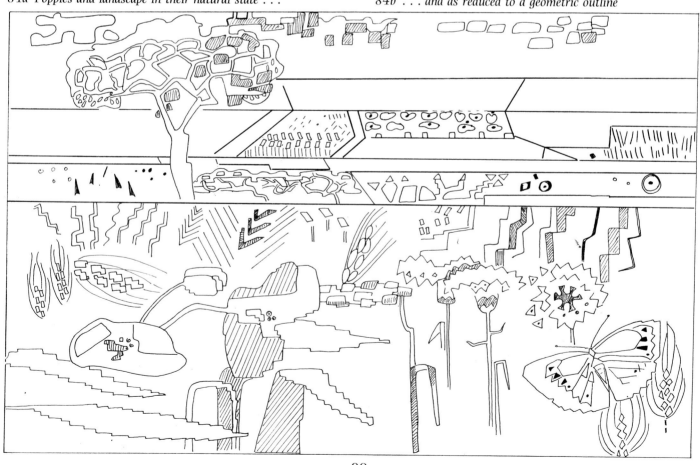

SUMMER COUNTRY FLOWER

· hand-knitted jacket ·

This jacket is hand-knitted for summer in a dazzling white yarn that looks like cotton. There are summer flower motifs in shades of pink, blue, and jade to knit in on the fronts, and a single poppy on the back. The jacket has large patch pockets and optional epaulettes.

Fig 85 shows the back poppy motif, the front of the jacket, and the left front in detail.

The motif charts are bold, so they are not too difficult to follow; but you could knit the jacket in plain white, and add some nautical buttons or braid. Or try knitting this shape for winter in Aran wool with a textured pattern.

· SIZE ·

To fit up to 101cm (40in) bust.

· MATERIALS ·

12-ply pure Spanish acrylic from Texere, shade card 297
850g (30oz) white, col A
75g (3oz) green, col B
125g (4¾oz) dark pink, col C
125g (4¾oz) light pink, col D
125g (4¾oz) blue, col E
1 pair each 4mm (US6 ENG8) and 5mm (US8 ENG6) needles
1 4½mm (US6 ENG7) circular needle
4 large porcelain buttons
4 small porcelain buttons
4 nylon snap fasteners
White cotton tape

· PATTERN NOTES ·

Work pattern motifs in stocking stitch, joining in and breaking off colours as required. A separate length of yarn is used for each motif, colours are linked to the next by twisting round each other on the wrong side to avoid holes.

· TENSION ·

17 sts and 24 rs to 10cm (4in) measured over patt motif on 5mm (US7 ENG6) ns.

· POCKET LININGS (2 alike) ·

Using 5mm (US7 ENG6) ns and A, COn 30 sts. K 40 rs in st st. Take off on a spare n.

· RIGHT FRONT ·

Using 4mm (US6 ENG8) ns and A, COn 54 sts. Work 8 rs in st st, beg with a P r.

Change to 5mm (US8 ENG6) ns. K 1 r to form foldline. Beg with a K r, work in st st, inc on left edge of work, as indicated on chart, until 39 rs have been worked, counting from above foldline, and ending with a K r.
R 40, WS: P 2, P 30 sts from pocket lining. Sl next 30 sts from right front onto st holder. P 24 to end of r.
R 41: K to end.

85 Summer country flower jacket design

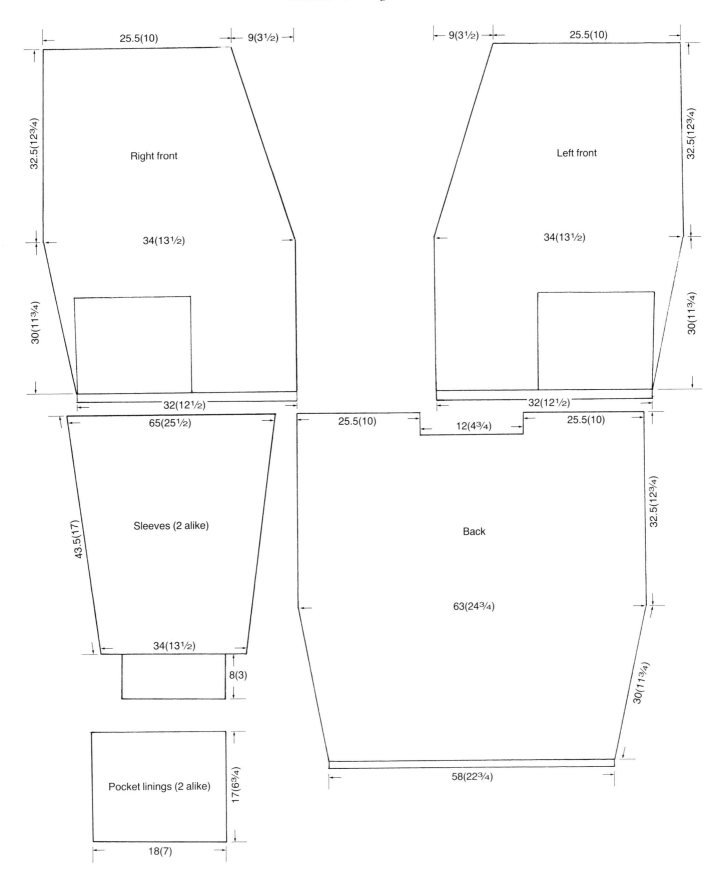

86 Summer country flower measurements

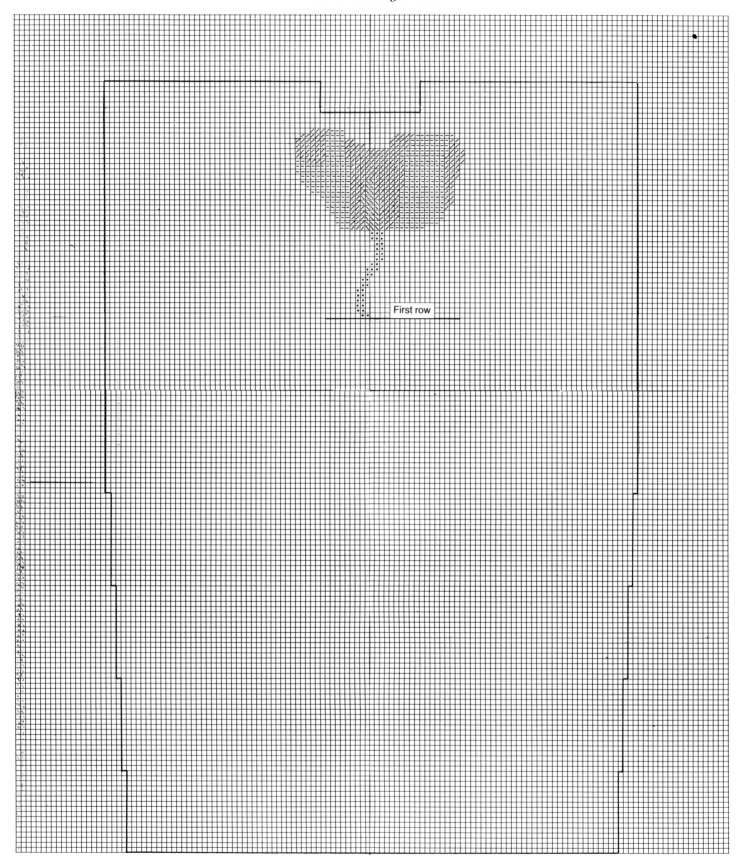

First row

87 *Summer country flower front motif. Begin work on a knit
row, having knitted hem and foldline row; knit in stocking
stitch*

R 42: P to end.
R 43: K 18A, K 4B, K 34A.
R 44: P 33A, P 6B, P 17A.

Cont in chart patt as set, inc as indicated until work measures 30cm (11¾in) from foldline (72 rs, 58 sts). Cont in st st, working straight on left of work, but dec on right for neck edge, as shown on chart. When work measures 62.5cm (24½in) from foldline (150 rs, 43 sts), leave sts on a spare n.

· LEFT FRONT ·

Work as given for right front, reversing shapings, and following patt motifs as shown on chart for left front.

· BACK ·

Using 4mm (US5 ENG8) ns and A, COn 98 sts. Work 8 rs, beg with a P row.

Change to 5mm (US7 ENG6) ns. K 1 r to form foldline. Work in st st, beg with a K r, inc on both sides of work as indicated on chart, until work is 30cm (11¾in), measured from above foldline (72 rs, 106 sts). Cont straight in st st until you reach patt motif on chart, ending with a P r.
Next r, r 105: K 53A, K 2B, K 51A.
R 106: P 50A, P 2B, P 54A.
Patt motif finishes on r 141 with a K r. Cont in st st to r 145.
Cast off for neck.
R 145: K 43; leave these sts on spare n.
CO loosely next 20 sts. K to end.
* Work 5 more rs on these rem 43 sts, beg with a P row *. Sl sts onto st holder. Return to those on spare n. Rep from * to *.

· SLEEVES (*2 alike*) ·

Using 4mm (US5 ENG8) ns and A, COn 44 sts. Work 21 rs (8cm, 3in) 1:1 rib.
R 22: K, inc 14 sts evenly across r (inc into the back of ev 3rd st, to last 2 sts, K 2) 58 sts.

Change to 5mm (US7 ENG6) ns and K in st st, at the same time inc 1 st at each end of the next and then ev foll 4th r until there are 110 sts. Cont straight until sleeve measures 43.5cm (17in) from top of rib (104 rs). CO.

· POCKET EDGINGS ·

With 4mm (US5 ENG8) ns and A, and with RS of work facing, K across 30 sts left on st holder at pocket opening, dec 6 sts evenly across r (K 3, K 2 tog to last 2 sts, then K 2 tog). 24 sts.

Work 4 more rs in st st, beg with a P r, K 1 r for foldline, then 4 rs st st, beg with a K r. CO.

· NECK AND FRONT FACING ·

Join shoulder seams. With a 4½mm (US6 ENG7) circular n, RS of work facing, and A, K evenly around edge of right front, neck of back, and down left front (106, 34, 106 = 246 sts).

K 4 rs of st st, beg with a P r. K 1 r for foldline. K 5 rs of st st, beg with a K r. CO.

· EPAULETTES (*2 alike; optional*) ·

Using 4mm (US5 ENG8) ns and A, COn 12 sts. Work 4 rs in 1:1 twisted rib (K into back of each K st).

· Buttonhole row ·

Rib 2, yarn round n, K 2 tog, rib 5, yarn round needle, K 2 tog, rib 2. Cont in twisted rib until whole piece measures 25.5cm (10in). CO.

· MAKING UP ·

Sew in ends on patt motifs and press all pieces with a warm iron (a quick light press on both sides of work, under a damp cloth).

Cut length of white cotton tape. Sew along shoulder seams to stabilize. Catch down pocket linings to WS of fronts. Catch down pocket edgings to WS, then hem tops on RS to neaten (this must be a firm stitch, or pockets will sag with use).

Set in sleeves, matching centre of CO edge to shoulder seams. Sew underarm and sleeve seams.

Fold hem to WS and sl st down.

Sew snap fasteners to left front border, one 3.5cm (1½in)

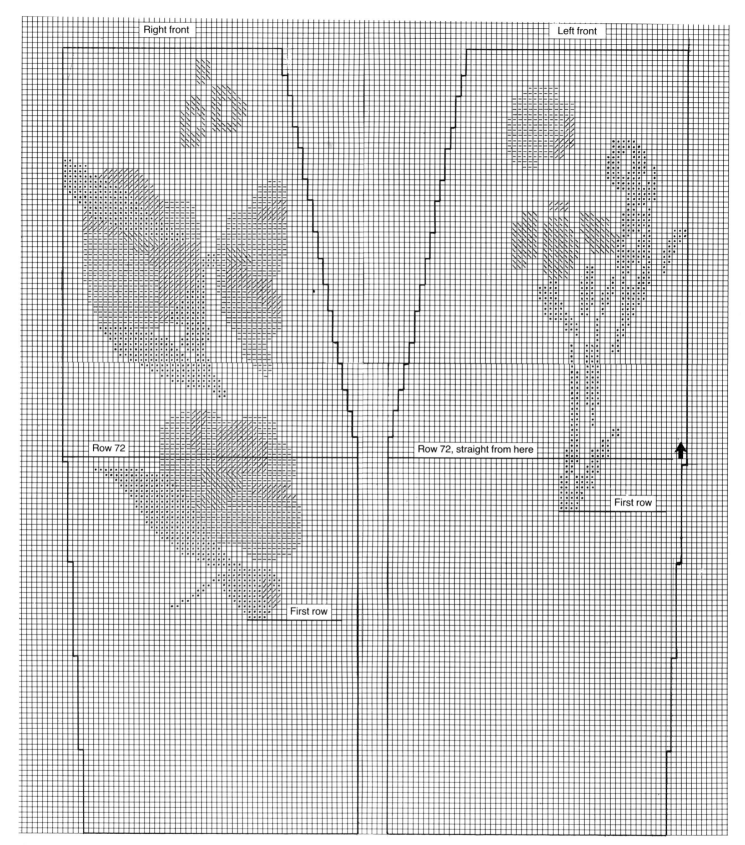

Right front

Left front

Row 72

Row 72, straight from here

First row

First row

above edge of hem, the others spaced 9cm (3½in) apart. Sew buttons on top of fasteners.

Sew CO edge of epaulettes at neck end, and catch down to mid-shoulder on seam. Position 2 small buttons below buttonholes at top of sleeve end.

88 Summer country flower back motif. Begin work on a knit row, having knitted hem and foldline.
Symbols on chart: A (blank), B (.), C (/), D (−) and E (\)

KNITTED DESIGNS FROM A POPPY SHAPE

Look at the poppy that the model is holding in her right hand (*Fig 89*), and you can see that the outline of the suit is that of the whole poppy. From the yoke down, it is knitted in soft pleats, and there is a wrapover effect on the skirt, and a poppy appliqué in silk on the side pocket.

Such an easy outline to a flower is perfect for any intarsia or Swiss darning work (shown to model's right); and it would be simple to reduce the shape to a geometric outline for punchcard motifs (shown to model's left).

Also shown is a poppy hat; beads and leather thongs used as a decorative centre on the poppy shape, and a poppy outline for beads and sequins.

· CHANGING THE PATTERN ·

You can knit the shape of the summer country flower jacket, but add different decorative effects. With the yarn left over from knitting the flower motifs, you can make sun tops, or summertime knitted accessories.

The couched effect is good on any knitted border as it is attractive to look at, and also reinforces the edge. Lay lengths of the background yarn along the border, and then make an over-and-over stitch that gathers the yarns at regular intervals. Use the same colour, but a different texture.

If the jacket is too baggy, gather tucks on the back piece, and finish with two buttons or fasteners.

· CHANGING THE STRUCTURE ·

For a more business-like appearance to the jacket, you could shorten the length, and add ties or a ribbed button inset on the garment front.

The knitted fabric for a jacket should be firm yet lightweight. Two that are knitted on a double-bed machine and that are suitable are described below.

· Style one ·

This is knitted on a Passap Duomatic. Use 3 strands of a fine lambswool in feeder 1, and contrast with either 1 strand of a superkid fine mohair, or 3 strands of the lambswool, but in a contrast colour. The needle set-up is shown in Diag 8.

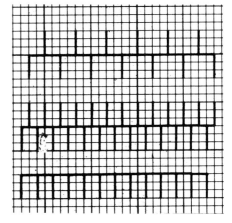

Diag 8 Needle set-up for style one

Handle down
Orange strippers
T4.3/4.2
BX↔/BX←
Deco card 11
Deco at 4
K 2 rs main yarn
K 2 rs contrast

· Style two ·

A finer fabric, again knitted on the Passap Duomatic, is a reversible jacquard, with the design shadowing through. The needle set-up is shown in Diag 9.

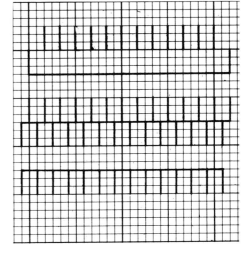

Diag 9 Needle set-up for style two

Handle down
Black strippers
T4.4/5.4
BX←/BX←
Deco card 10
Deco at 4
K 2 rs 2 strands lambswool
K 2 rs 1 strand mohair

· **D**RYSTONE WALL PATTERN ·

On a single-bed machine use any Fair Isle pattern with short floats on the reverse side of the work. The drystone wall pattern is ideal. Try a 4- or 3-ply camel hair in feeder 1, and 2 strands of cream or white superkid mohair in feeder 2. Blend wool with silk, alpaca and cashmere, as these yarns represent luxury and elegance, though the softness of the fabric is all-important.

You'll find that a small surface variant in pattern is perfect for this type of garment. You don't want bulk; and a big Fair Isle pattern or a tucked stitch is unattractive on a fuller figure, and would swamp a small one.

· **F**AIR ISLE BORDER ·

If you want to keep the basic shape of the jacket, but would like to replace the flower pattern with something equally colourful, you could have a Fair Isle border. It is a good idea to use lots of contrasting colours, so you can wear it with almost anything.

On a machine-knitted version of the jacket, you could knit the border separately and then sew it on, or use 2 positioning pins (or whatever method you use for single motif work) – one on the edge, and one about 13 needles in from both front edges – and any Fair Isle pattern. In this way the machine will knit pattern on just the border, and plain on the rest of the knitting.

89 Knitted designs from poppy shape

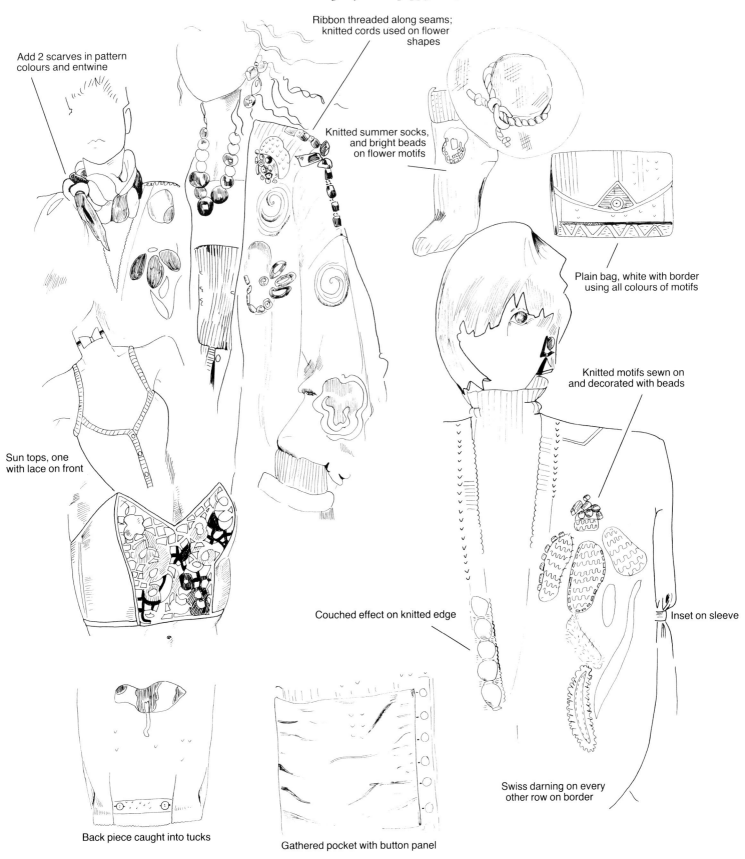

Add 2 scarves in pattern colours and entwine

Ribbon threaded along seams; knitted cords used on flower shapes

Knitted summer socks, and bright beads on flower motifs

Plain bag, white with border using all colours of motifs

Knitted motifs sewn on and decorated with beads

Sun tops, one with lace on front

Couched effect on knitted edge

Inset on sleeve

Swiss darning on every other row on border

Back piece caught into tucks

Gathered pocket with button panel

90 Summer country flower jacket – changing pattern

91 Summer country flower, using the same shape but making structural changes

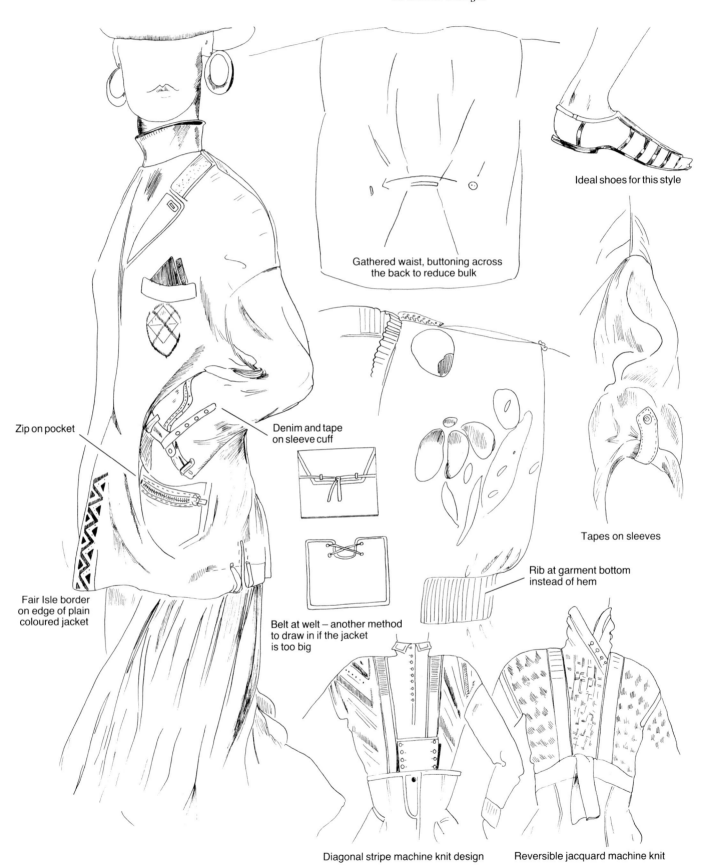

Ideal shoes for this style

Gathered waist, buttoning across the back to reduce bulk

Zip on pocket

Denim and tape on sleeve cuff

Tapes on sleeves

Fair Isle border on edge of plain coloured jacket

Belt at welt – another method to draw in if the jacket is too big

Rib at garment bottom instead of hem

Diagonal stripe machine knit design

Reversible jacquard machine knit

AUTUMN

92 *Geranium and nasturtium leaves*

By October, there are only a few flowers left, though the colours and the shape of the leaves, particularly on geraniums and nasturtiums, stand out (*Fig 92*).

Autumn is the time for preparing the land for sewing seeds (*Fig 93*). There are the bright colours of the hips and berries, and these make a lovely collection when they are put together in a vase (*Fig 94*).

93 *The sights of autumn*

Bryony

Sloes

Hawthorn or May

Blackberries   Elderberries

94 *Autumn hedge collection*

103

There are some flowers left in the garden (*Fig 95*); the iris
would be an ideal intarsia design in mohairs (*Fig 96*).

95 *Late summer flowers*

96 Iris mohair sweater

LOOSE FITTING AND LONG

· machine-knitted sweater ·

This machine-knitted jumper has animals motifs on both back and front. It has a narrow stand-up collar, and different motifs in Fair Isle patterning on the collar, sleeve top, cuff, and welt bands. It is ideal for the chill November winds.

· SIZES ·

To fit 81–96(101–106)cm, 32–38(40–42)in bust.

· MATERIALS ·

Nethy's pure Shetland wool
475 (550)g, 17(19½)oz, Perth green, ref 1591, col A
150 (200)g, 5½(7¼)oz, dark grey, ref 242, col B
75 (100)g, 3(3¾)oz, silver grey, ref 983, col C

· MACHINES ·

These instructions are written for a standard gauge punchcard machine, with a 24 stitch repeat.

· PATTERN NOTES ·

Front and back garment pieces are knitted from side seam to side seam, rather than from welt to shoulder seam, with 7 complete pattern motifs over width of machine.

Sleeves are knitted from top down, towards cuff. For Picot, transfer alternate stitches to adjacent needles, leaving all needles in WP.

Punchcard patterns (punch cards before starting to knit): A – animal motif; B – neckband; C – top of sleeve; D – cuffs and welts.

· TENSION ·

30 sts and 36 rs to 10cm (4in) measured over patt (T8.2 approx).

· FRONT AND BACK (alike) ·

Push 86 ns at left and 86 ns at right of centre 0 to WP (172ns). Mark n20 on right of 0. Using MT and A, COn and K a few rs, ending with carriage at right. Insert patt card A, lock on starter r. RC000. A, K 9 (19) rs. Machine on left (preselection r), set carriage for patterning Fair Isle.

K 1 r to right. B in feeder 2. Release card and cont in Fair Isle to RC60(70). Change to C in feeder 2. RC62(72). Mark right-hand seam edge (for neck). Cont in Fair Isle to RC115(125) (machine on left). Change col in feeder 2 to B.

RC140(150). Mark right-hand seam edge. Cont patterning to RC192(202); patt finishes. Set carriage to K plain. Col A in feeder 1, MT, K 10 (20) rs in st st. RC 202(222). Mark n 20 on right of 0. Using A, K a few rs and release from machine.

· NECKBAND (2 alike) ·

Push up 60 ns to WP. With WS facing, pick up sts along front neck seam line, between neck markers, and replace onto ns. Bring up 1 n at each end (62 sts).

RC000, using A, T10, K to left. Insert patt card B and lock on starter row. Set carriage to patt Fair Isle. MT, K to right. B in feeder 2. Release card, K in patt to RC12. Remove card and B. Set carriage to K plain. K 1 r to left. Transfer sts for Picot. K in st st to RC 28. Using WY, K a few rs and release from machine.

Rep for back.

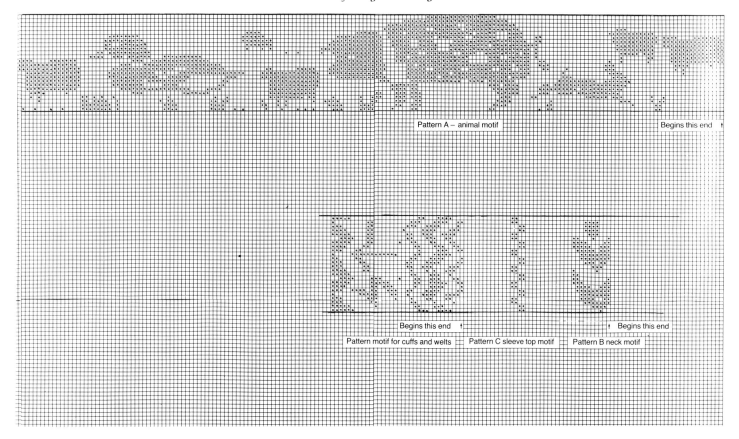

Pattern A – animal motif   Begins this end †

Begins this end †   † Begins this end

Pattern motif for cuffs and welts   Pattern C sleeve top motif   Pattern B neck motif

97 *Loose-fitting and long charts*

· SLEEVES (*2 alike*) ·

Join neckband and shoulder seams. Push up 132 ns to WP. With WS facing, with shoulder seam at centre 0 n, and picking up from between markers, replace sts from joined front and back pieces onto ns. Bring up 1 n at each end (134 sts).

RC000. Insert patt card C in machine and lock on starter r. Using A, MT, K to left. Set carriage to patterning Fair Isle. K to right. With C in feeder 2, release card and cont in Fair Isle to RC6. Set carriage to K plain. A in feeder 1. K in st st to RC120(144). Using WY, K a few rs and release from machine.

· CUFFS (*2 alike*) ·

Push 68 ns to WP. With WS of work facing, replace sts from cuff end of work just taken off machine, with 2 sts onto each n (the first and last n will have 1 st). Bring up 1 n at both ends (70 sts). Pull out all ns to E position. RC000.

Insert patt D and lock on starter r. Using A, T10, K to left. Set carriage to patterning Fair Isle. MT, K to right. With B in feeder 2, release patt and cont in Fair Isle to RC36. Remove card and B. Set carriage to K plain. K to left. Transfer sts for Picot. T7, K in st st to RC76. Using WY, K a few rs and release from machine.

· WELTS (*2 alike*) ·

Pick up first from front garment piece, then from back. Push up 156 (170) ns to WP. With WS facing, pick up sts along welt seam edge and replace onto ns. Bring up 1 n at both ends, 158 (172) ns. Pull out all ns to E position. RC000.

Insert patt D in machine and lock on starter r. Using A, T10, K to left. Set carriage to patterning Fair Isle. MT, K to right. With B in feeder 2, release card and cont in Fair Isle to RC36. Set carriage to K plain. Remove card and B in feeder 2. A in feeder 1, K 1 r to left. Transfer sts for Picot. T7, K in st st to RC76. Using WY, K a few rs and release from machine. Rep for back.

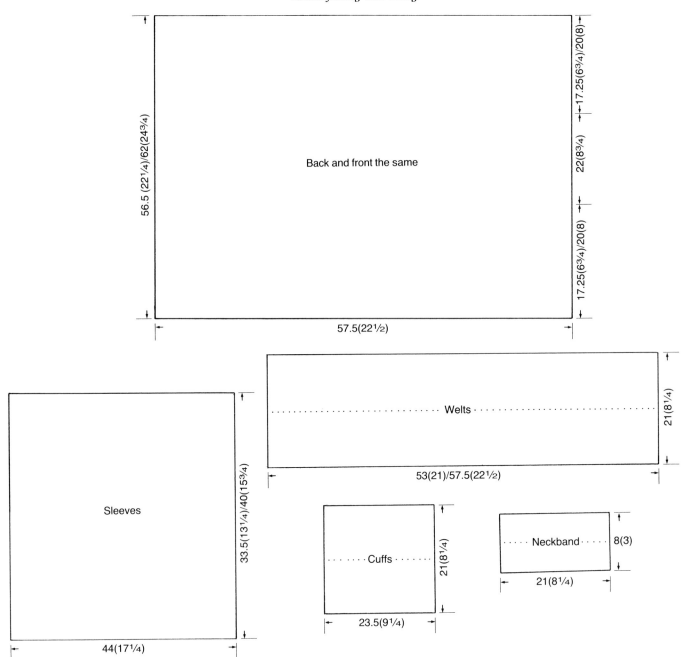

Back and front the same

56.5 (22¹/₄)/62 (24³/₄)

17.25 (6³/₄)/20 (8)

22 (8³/₄)

17.25 (6³/₄)/20 (8)

57.5 (22¹/₂)

Sleeves

33.5 (13¹/₄)/40 (15³/₄)

44 (17¹/₄)

Welts

21 (8¹/₄)

53 (21)/57.5 (22¹/₂)

Cuffs

21 (8¹/₄)

23.5 (9¹/₄)

Neckband

8 (3)

21 (8¹/₄)

98 *Loose-fitting and long measurements*

99 Loose-fitting and long design

Leather buttons

Suitable
pocket top

Wooden jewellery
looks good with
outdoor jumper

Silver
scroll-look buttons

A cartridge belt feature
on pocket

The design using:
Leather patches

Nautical look

Cowboy

Paper fasteners
used as studs

More leather patches

Nautical
button

*100 Loose-fitting and long – how the design is associated with
outdoors*

· UNDERARM GUSSETS (*2 alike*) ·

RC000. COn 2 sts by 'e' loop method. MT, with A, K to left and return to right. * Bring up 2 ns to make a new st at both ends, K to left and then right *. Rep from * to * 9 times (20 sts). RC20. Dec 1 st at both ends on next and ev foll alt r 9 times. RC38. CO rem 2 sts.

· MAKING UP ·

Sew in ends. Press all pieces on WS of knitting, under a damp cloth with a hot iron setting. On front and back pieces, it is important to press work in the direction of the knitting.

The sweater has a ridged 'inside-out' seam feature on side seams. To do this, with a knitting n, pick sts on front and back sides; using a double thickness of A, with reverse sides facing each other, CO sts tog. Do this from welt end up to armhole; the last 12 sts on both pieces are CO singly. This is to allow the underarm gusset to be sewn in. To do this, place point on gusset at seam, then sew each of the 2 sides of diamond with each edge of sleeve; continue to sew to Picot line on cuff. Fold cuffs to inside and catch down sts. Sew welt seams tog at both sides, fold to inside along Picot line, and catch down sts. Fold collar to inside, catch down sts.

· THE DESIGN ·

The way the animal motifs follow each other across the knitting gives the impression of shapes taken from a tapestry, where the little figures would be filled in with different yarns in various embroidery stitches. In Fig 99, which shows where the idea for the design first came from, the animals look almost as though they are leaping from square to square on a checker board. The small check pattern on the sleeve top is a good, solid contrast to the rather irregular shapes of the animals.

The motif pattern on the neck comes from the shape of an ear of corn, and there is a more geometric outline of the plant and leaves for the cuff and welt motif. The pattern of a duck's feathers can also look like this outline, when they are seen in a mass.

Fig 100 shows how the style of the jumper is associated with the outdoors. There are rocks, stone walls and rough surfaces. Wool is a lovely natural yarn, and, as it comes from the fleece of a sheep, it has a natural affinity with other natural surfaces such as leather, wood and bone.

In the first design for the original shape there are leather patches sewn on the shoulders and elbows, and there is a mock cartridge belt feature on the top of a pocket. The patches would prolong the life of the design, as a working sweater could wear at the elbows; but make sure you use a washable or chamois leather to combine with the wool, and sew them on to the garment with a sewing machine using a zigzag stitch.

The second design is a sailing sweater. You could knit cable strips, or cords to look like rope braids, and decorate with gilt buttons.

For the cowboy look in the third sketch, fringing has been sewn onto the yoke. This could be purchased leather fringing, knitted fringing made on the machine, or fine knitted cord caught down in loops and sewn along the yoke seam line.

In the last design, the leather shoulder pads have been attached to the knitting with paper fasteners. It is a good idea to tack down a lining to the patch, or the two prongs on the fastener which are opened could be uncomfortable. The welt has been left open at both sides and a leather buckle sewn on.

Sometimes, if you mix a completely contrasting fabric with wool the effect is good, and this style of jumper worn over a long, full lace skirt could look stunning.

Fig 101 shows some ideas for knitting up the same shape, but changing the yarn. The design on the left is knitted in cotton, and has lace panels or braid inserted on the shoulder seams. Any sort of hand-transferred lace pattern will look good knitted in a cotton yarn.

The pattern on the knitted skirt is made by transferring every 6th stitch onto its adjacent needle, either to the right or left. Leave all needles in the working position. Knit 7 rows. Repeat these three steps again, moving the pattern along so that every hole is placed exactly half-way between each 2 holes of the previous pattern row. When following a hand knitting pattern, this is equivalent to wl fwd, K 2 tog.

A very easy and effective-looking braid, shown in the sketch on the welt of the cotton top, is simply a length of knitting gathered into loops, and then fastened through the loops with a yarn in the same colour, but of a different texture. This is also a good method of holding down a hem that may want to curl.

In the sketch on the right, the long jumper has been caught in with a wide, soft leather belt. This time the stitches are textured, with fur and knitted strips sewn on.

A long-line sweater is one of the easiest shapes to wear, as it elongates a round figure, and slims down a big bust. If

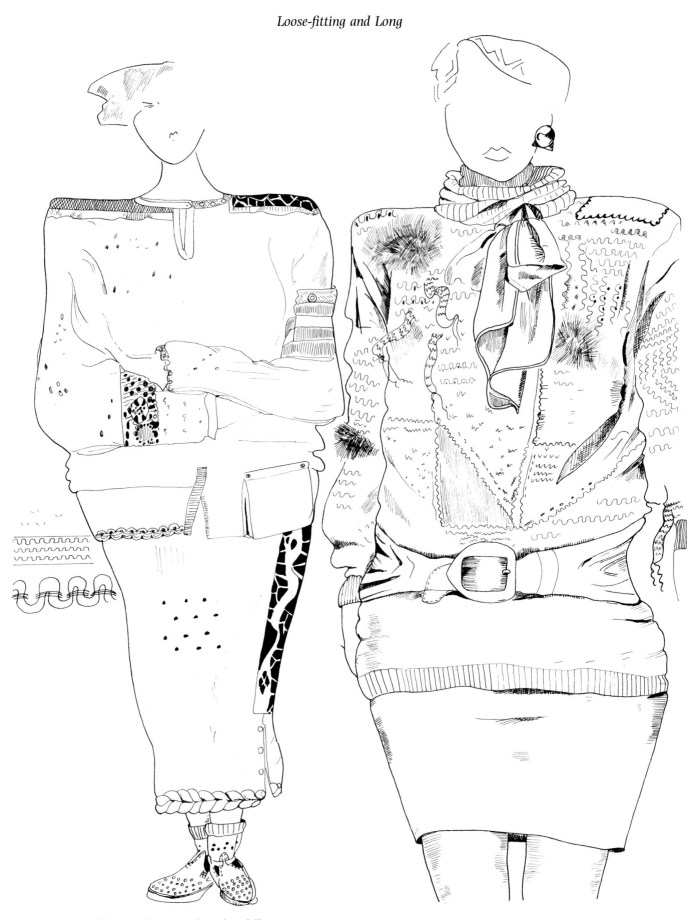

101 Loose-fitting and long – the same shape but different yarns

102 Loose-fitting and long – ways to change the shape

you have large hips, don't let the welt fall at hip level, or you will draw attention to your most bulky area.

In Fig 102 the theme for the sweater is still the outdoors. It is interesting how textural wool is in its natural state, with its twists and kinks. We can see how closely the bark on a tree, or lichen on stones, can resemble these textures. In these designs, the sweater is knitted without the Fair Isle patterning on the front and back. In the first design, the welt has been replaced by ribbing, and wooden beads; hand-transferred lace stitches, and knitted strips are added. In the next design there are blocks of knitting in various textured yarns, in the same colour as the background, but changing the yarn.

A man may shy away from the animal motifs, and so another variation on the design is to knit it in stocking stitch, with a ribbed welt, over-stitching on the shoulder and sleeve tops seams, and a high ribbed collar. Add leather oval-shaped patches, with a half-belt on the front.

Leather can also be used to thong a sleeve, in a diamond-shaped pattern, or it can be threaded through in short diagonals and then tied and held with a wooden button or bead. You can also use a laced-up feature on the welt and side seams, if you find the style too loose.

In the final sketch the knitted fabric on the front piece is gathered and these gathers are made into a feature, caught down with buttons and bar button loops.

103 Mountain pass

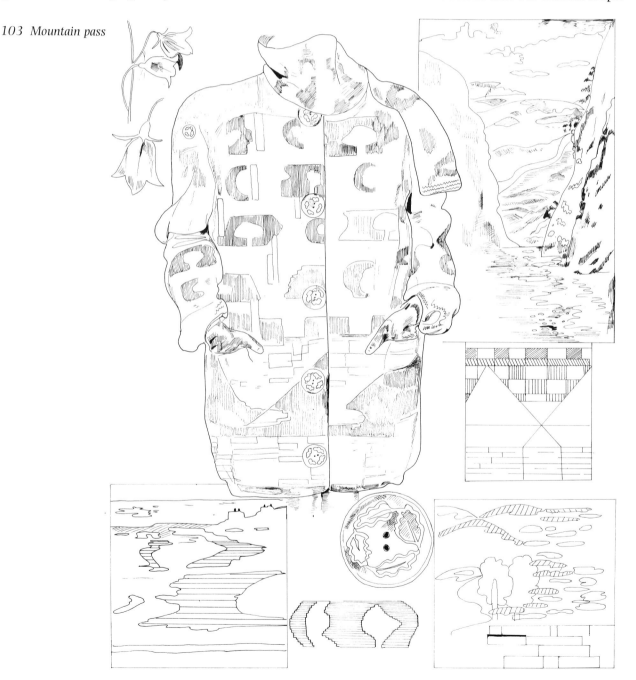

The mountain pass design is an idea for a knitted coat (*Fig 103*). Again, mountains and a river are the source of inspiration. Fig 104 shows how the creek was reduced for an overall pattern. The blocks of colour represent changes of colour, rather as one would find in an Impressionist painting.

First row

104 Mountain pass chart. Suggested colours: (blank) white; (-) black; (\\) green; (/) blue; (+) pink; (.) yellow.

You can see how a muff in looped knitting would be an ideal accessory, just as leather ties would be. You can plait the leather, cutting three groups of three lengths in a soft leather, and then plaiting them together.

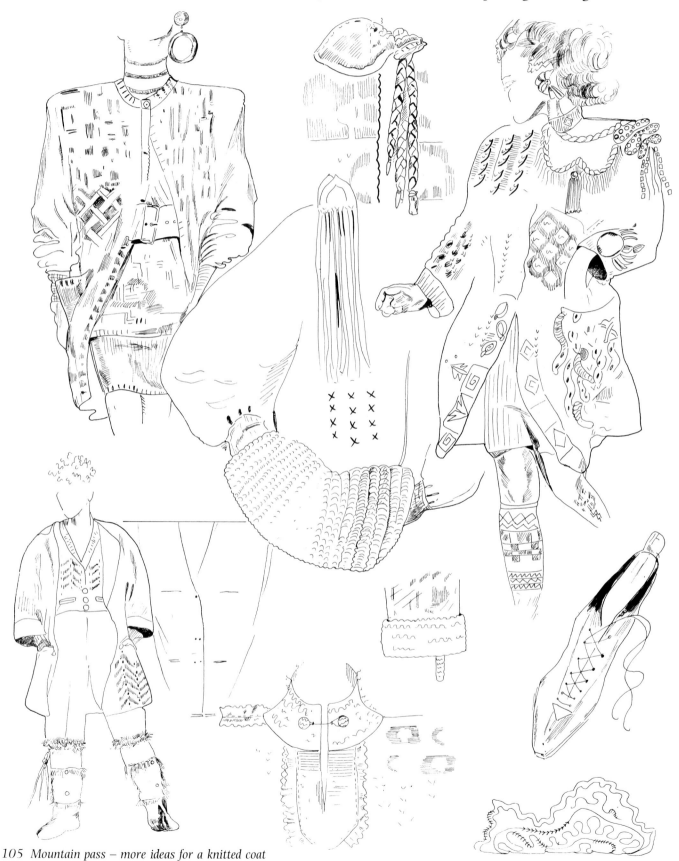

105 Mountain pass – more ideas for a knitted coat

WINTER

Now it is winter and the larder is full. Jars of preserves stand on the shelves, and there is a jug of sloe gin and a bottle of dandelion wine.

106 Larder full in winter

107 *Flight pattern design*

118

FLIGHT PATTERN

· hand-knitted sweater ·

This huge, roomy sweater will suit both men and women. It looks and feels good, and is hand-knitted in a soft, warm chunky Icelantic wool in the most beautiful subtle colours. There is a gently draped neckline in a V-shape that crosses over itself at the front. The stunning bird pattern that spans the whole of the back takes time and concentration to knit, but is certainly worth the effort.

The design began as a sketch of ivy leaves toppling over a drystone wall, and then developed into feather patterns (*Fig 108*). The pattern stands out particularly well as the outline stitches in the Icelantic wool are in black, while the bird's head is knitted in black angora. The sleeves are knitted in the cream background colour. There is just a small feather motif on the front. The collar, cuffs and welt are knitted in a firm garter stitch that keeps the sweater in shape perfectly.

· SIZE ·

One size that will fit up to 106cm (42in) bust in a loose-fitting style.

· MATERIALS ·

Yarns from Texere; Icelantic-type wool
800g (28¼oz) white, col A
100g (3¾oz) blue, col B
200g (7¼oz) black, col C
300g (10¾oz) purple lovat, col D
100g (3¾oz) beige, col E
20g (1oz) angora, black, *used double*, col F
1 pair each 5½mm (US8 ENG5) and 7mm (US10 ENG2) ns

· PATTERN NOTE ·

Chart is worked in stocking stitch, beginning with a knit row. Join in and break off colours as required. Use separate lengths of yarn for each motif. Link one colour to the next by twisting them around each other on the wrong side; this will avoid gaps.

· TENSION ·

14 sts and 18 rs to 10cm (4in) measured over st st on 7mm (US10 ENG2) ns.

· FRONT ·

Using 5½ mm (US8 ENG5) ns and D COn 88 sts. Work 6.5cm (2¾in) or 20 rs of firm garter st (K into the back of ev st)*.

Change to 7mm (US10 ENG2) ns and A, and work in st st to r 52, counting from top of garter st. Mark each end of r for underarm.

Cont in st st in A until r 61, ending with a WS r. Commence patt from chart, using separate balls of yarn for each col, and twisting yarns between cols to avoid holes. *At the same time:*

· Divide for neck ·

Next r: K 11A, K 13C, K 20A, turn, leaving rem sts on a spare n, and cont on these sts only for left side of front.
Next r: CO 1 st, P 16A, P 20C, P 7A.
Cont dec where indicated on chart, and working from motif chart. When motif finished, cont in st st and A until 104 rs, counting from top of garter st, have been worked, ending with a K r. CO.

With RS facing, return to sts on spare n. Rejoin yarn. K 2

108 *Flight pattern – birds from the leaves*

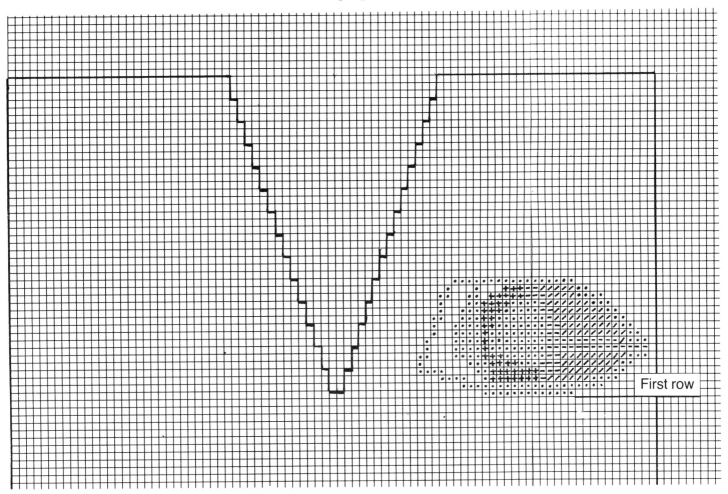

First row

109 *Flight pattern front motif. First row starts on row 62 of*
knitting.
Symbols on chart: A (blank), B (/), C (.), D (+) and
E (−)

sts tog, K to end of r. Complete RS to match left, omitting
patt motif.

· BACK ·

Work as given for the front of the sweater to *. Change to
7mm (US10 ENG2) ns. Commence patt from chart, using
separate balls and working as before, as follows:
R 1, RS: K 8A, K 2C, K 78A.
R 2: P 77A, P 3C, P 5A, P 1C, P 1A, P 1C.
Cont working from chart until 104 rs completed, counting
from top of garter st, ending with a K r and marking each
end of r 52 for underarm (counting from top of garter st).
CO.

· SLEEVES · (2 alike) ·

Using 5½mm (US8 ENG5) ns and D, COn 46 sts. Work
6.5cm (2¾in), 20 rs, of firm garter st. Change to 7mm
(US10 ENG2) ns and A, and K in st st, inc 1 st at each end
of this r and then ev foll 4th r until 82 sts on ns. K straight
in st st until 76 rs worked, counting from top of garter st.
CO.

· COLLAR ·

Using 5½mm (US8 ENG5) ns and D, COn 150 sts. Work 26
rs in firm garter st. CO. Mark centre st (to match with
centre of back of neck when sewing up).

First row ↓

110 *Flight pattern back motif. First row starts immediately after welt of firm garter stitch*
Symbols on chart: A (blank), B (/), C (.), D (+), E (−) and F (\)

122

Flight pattern

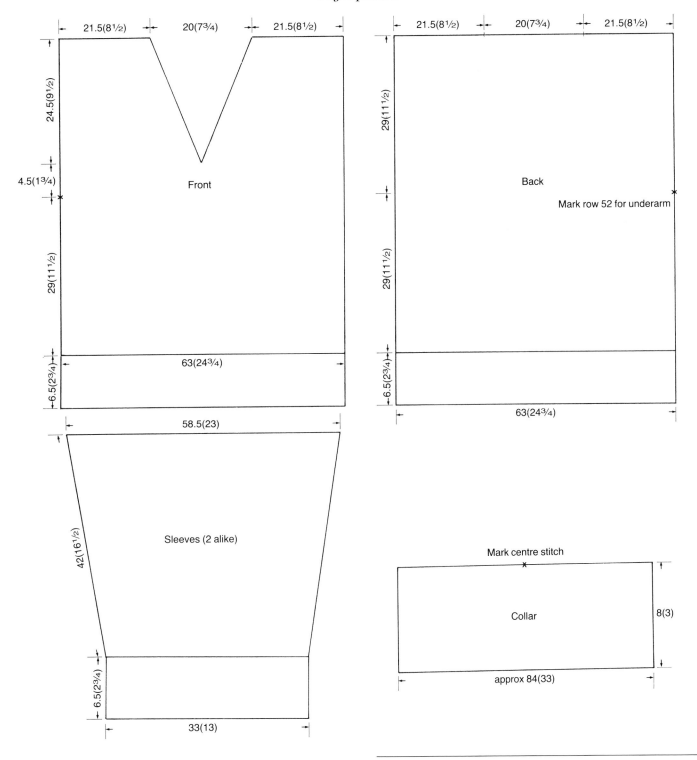

111 *Flight pattern measurements*

· MAKING UP ·

Join shoulder seams. Set sleeves in flat, matching centre of CO edge of sleeve to shoulder seam. Join side and sleeve seams.

Sew collar to neck edge, matching centre of back neck to collar mark, and sew down to V of front, overlapping the two edges.

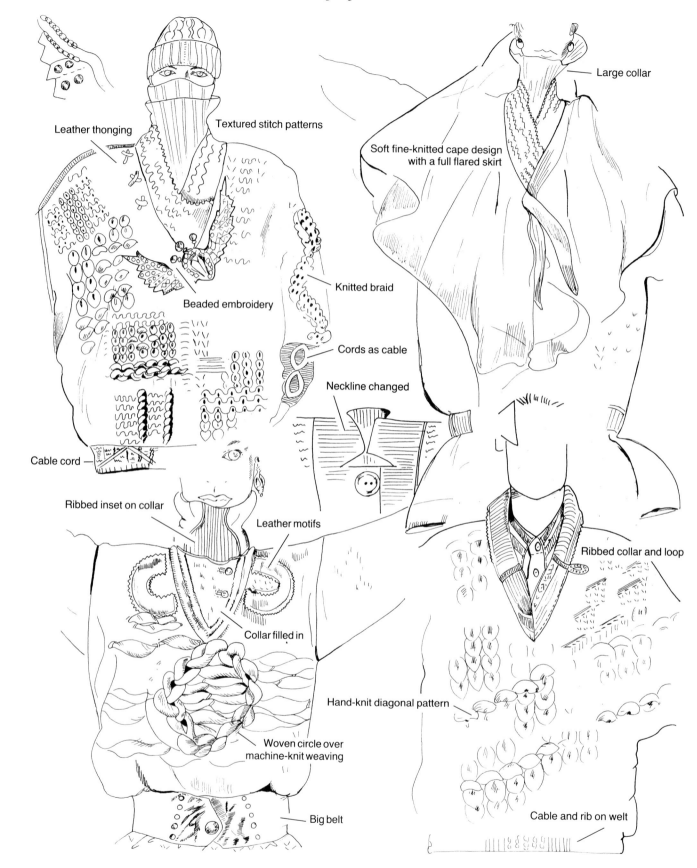

Leather thonging

Textured stitch patterns

Large collar

Soft fine-knitted cape design with a full flared skirt

Knitted braid

Beaded embroidery

Cords as cable

Neckline changed

Cable cord

Ribbed inset on collar

Leather motifs

Ribbed collar and loop

Collar filled in

Hand-knit diagonal pattern

Woven circle over machine-knit weaving

Big belt

Cable and rib on welt

112 *Flight pattern – ideas for designs you can knit to sweater shape*

· THE DESIGN, AND VARIATIONS ·

The loose-fitting style of this sweater is a very easy shape for all figures to wear, as it skims over every bump, and it's long enough for the bulkiness of the design not to give a dumpy look. As the shape is straight, it would be simple to cut down the size of the width measurement (that is, the number of stitches you cast on for the front and back pieces), if you feel it would be just too big for you. (This applies if you were knitting the flight pattern sweater in a different stitch, and not using the bird motif on the back.)

If you are not sure what to take off, here are some approximate guidelines.

Should you want *a very close fitting* effect to any jumper, you would take off 5cm (2in) from the total body measurement. For instance, for a person who has a bust size of 91cm (36in), make your sweater to a bust measurement of 86cm (34in), and you will get a very clingy, body-hugging effect.

For a *close fitting*, with a smooth contour over the body, add 3cm (1¼in).

A *standard fitting*, normal body-skimming effect is achieved by adding 5cm (2in) to your bust size.

For a *straight-hanging* sweater, add 10cm (4in).

For an *oversized* effect, you should add as much as 14cm (5½in) or more to your bust measurement (that is, for a person with a 91cm (36in) bust, knit a sweater with an overall bust measurement of 104cm (41in) or more.

Use any textured stitch pattern for this style. Machine knitters should try tuck and slip stitch patterns. Suitable hand-knit patterns to try are given below. The asterisks in the first four patterns indicate parts of pattern to be repeated should the design be enlarged.

Basket stitch
COn multiples of 9, plus 2, plus the edge st (or selvedge).
Rs 1 and 7: * P 2, K 7,* P 2.
Rs 2, 6 and 8: P.
Rs 3 and 5: * P 2, K 3, P 1, K 3, * P 2.
R 4: P 2, * P 2, K 1, P 1, K 1, P 4 *.

Garter stitch check
Multiple of 20 sts.
Rs 1 and 3: * P 10, K 10 *.
Rs 2 and 4: * P 10, K 10 *.
R 5: K.
Rs 6 and 8: * K 10, P 10 *.
Rs 7 and 9: * K 10, P 10 *.
R 10: P.

Ribbed garter stitch
R 1, WS: * K 3, yarn over n, sl 1 *.
R 2: all K, working tog through back of loops the sl st and the yarn over n before it.

Rectangular checks
Multiples of 6 sts.
R 1 and alt rs: K.
Rs 2, 4, 6, 8, 10 and 12: * K 3, P 3 *.
Rs 14, 16, 18, 20, 22 and 24: * P 3, K 3 *.

Diagonal pattern
Multiples of 8 sts.
R 1, RS: * K 6, P 2 *; rep from * to *.
R 2: P 1, * K 2, P 6 *; rep from * to * ending K 2, P 5.
R 3: K 4, * P 2, K 6 *; rep from * to * ending P 2, K 2.
R 4: P 3, * K 2, P 6 *; rep from * to * ending K 2, P 3.
R 5: K 2, * P 2, K 6 *; rep from * to * ending P 2, K 4.
R 6: P all sts.
These 6 rs form 1 patt.

The machine-knitted design in Fig 112 shows leather motifs sewn onto a cream, woven stitch background. The background yarn used is a fine slub cotton in parchment, and the weaving yarn is a thick cream Icelantic wool. Later, outlines in a square or circle shape to an approximate measurement of 7cm (2¾in) are sewn on by hand, using chain stitch worked in the Icelantic wool. Add a cross stitch in the centre of the square, or an ivory or wooden bead.

KNOT GARDEN

· machine-knitted bag ·

This very large carpet-bag style knitted bag takes a long time to knit, but is well worth the effort. It is used as an intarsia design, knitted on a Knitmaster Chunky 120, but you could hand-knit the design just as well. There are no difficult calculations involved, as this is just a straight length of knitting that is folded over in two.

The design is of flower heads and leaves that are enclosed by circles and loops, inspired by a knot garden – one of those box-edged Elizabethan gardens that are so delightful. The colours used are beautiful, ranging from a deep plum with its lighter tone of a pinky/peach, to shades of green, and flashes of a bright buttercup yellow.

Fig 113 shows both sides of the bag, and also the designs for both small and large buttons.

The bag has masses of space inside, with a centre pocket made of simulated leather, and two further inside pockets which are closed lengthwise with a piece of snap tape. There are six small knitted pockets attached on the outside of the bag, three at each end, one below the other. These have oval-shaped porcelain buttons with a flower head design worked on them, and the button is sewn to the little flap on the pocket, which would be ideal for holding something small like a comb or pen. There are three large flaps positioned along the top of the bag, that can close it on the opposite side with a popper. These, again, are decorated with a larger design of the porcelain buttons. This larger button picks out perfectly one of the knitted motifs on the bag.

There is a knitted woven braid that is used as a handle for the bag; this involves another technique for the machine knitter.

· SIZE ·

Approx width 54cm (21¼in); approx length 36cm (14¼in).

· MATERIALS ·

Chunky pure new wool by Texere; shade card 267.
600g (21¼oz) dark green, ref 586, col A
200g (7¼oz) berry, ref 486, col B
100g (3¾oz) delph, ref 786, col C
300g (10¾oz) buttercup, col D
300g (10¾oz) plum, col E
200g (7¼oz) light wood green, col F
100g (3¾oz) sand, col G
100g (3¾oz) white, col H
Simulated leather, colour burgundy, ref LM 184, approx 70cm (27½in) × 56cm (22in) from Kersen Ltd
Approx 1m (39in) snap tape in navy
3 large, 6 small porcelain buttons
1 remnant for inside pockets, suggested fabric is tapestry type material, 120cm (47¼in) × 49cm (19¼in).
Binding for covering seams.
Approx 1.5m (59in), 6cm (2½in) wide braid for handle (if you are not making your own).
3 large press fasteners.

· MACHINE ·

Knitted on Knitmaster Chunky 120.

· PATTERN NOTES ·

To help you follow the chart, have it enlarged and then use coloured pencils to fill in the squares that match your yarn colours; or it may be worth copying out the whole chart onto large-squared graph paper, and then colouring it in. A separate supply of yarn is needed for each block of colour to be knitted across the row. The same colour often occurs more than once in a single row, but the same yarn supply cannot be used, so you will need as many balls as there are blocks of that colour.

113 Knot garden design

114 Knot garden intarsia chart
Symbols on chart: A (blank), B (|), C (\), D (/), E (.),
F (X), G (−) and H (+)

128

· TENSION ·

18 sts and 26 rs to 10cm (4in) measured over intarsia patt (T6 approx).

· KNITTED PIECE ·

COn by 'e' loop method over 110 sts in A. K 6 rs. Change to intarsia carriage and follow chart to end of design. Remove intarsia carriage and K 6 rs with A. CO.

Small pockets (six alike)
Push 12 ns to WP. COn 'e' loop method in A. K straight to RC18. Break yarn. K several rs of WK and release from machine. Turn work. Carr on the right. Replace on machine. Rejoin A. RC000. K 1 r at T10 (folding row). T6, K to right.

With 3-prong transfer tool, CO 2 sts at both ends, and rep on next alt r (4 sts remain). K 2 rs. CO.

· KNITTED BRAID FOR HANDLE ·
· (optional) ·

Knitted on Brother KH-830. Knit 2 pieces alike.

Insert PC 1 in machine or use similar 1 × 1 patt. COn by hand over 120 ns, with a dark green 4-ply yarn. RC000. T8. K to RC3. Carr on left. Set machine for weaving. K to right.

Using knot garden chunky cols, and changing cols on alt rs, weave to RC26. With 4-ply only, K 23 rs at T8. K 1 r at T10. CO.

· MAKING UP BRAID ·

Sew 2 pieces of braid tog. Sew long edges of work, woven side of patt facing you. Turn tube inside. Press, stiffen with interfacing or skirt petersham if you wish (braid has the woven side as inside).

· KNITTED CLASPS (3 alike) ·

Bring up 14 ns on machine bed to WP, then leave 1 n in NWP, and bring up another 14 ns to WP. COn 'e' loop method.

With A, T5, K to RC34. Carr on right. Counting from left, pull out ev 3rd n to E position (i.e. ns 1 and 2 in WP, 3 in NWP, ns 4 and 5 in WP, n 6 in NWP, along the row from left to right; and also repeating for ns beyond the central n that has been in NWP all the time).

Set machine so it won't knit those in HP. K 4 rs. RC38, K all sts. K straight to RC40. CO.

With RS tog, sew along long edges and turn to RS. Sew ends tog. Sew tucked end of clasp, evenly spaced with the two other clasps, to top of bag.

· MAKING UP BAG ·

Fold the 6 rs on COn and CO edges to WS and hem down. Cut out leather lining to measurements. Turn AB, CD 2cm (¾in) to WS and sew down. On knitted piece, turn the width of 9 sts in on both side edges to WS and tack down.

Fold the length of knitting in half; mark this line with tacking (XY) on knitted piece. Count 22 rs down from both CO and COn edges. Mark. Do this on both sides.

Match centre line and pinning between marks. Put WS of lining to WS of knitted piece (you will bend back facing on knitted piece). Sew tog on both sides with 1cm (½in) stitching line.

Turn whole bag, so that seams just sewn are now facing you (i.e. RS of lining now showing outwards). Sew with whip stitch the knitted seam line, to both ends of lining. Bind all seams to neaten.

· MAKING AND ATTACHING ·
· INNER FLAP POCKETS ·

Cut a piece of material 120cm (47¼in) long × 49cm (19¼in) wide. Fold in half and cut across the width so that you have 2 pieces, both 60cm (23¾in) × 49cm (19¼). Fold each piece again to 30cm (11¾in) × 49cm (19¼in). With WS tog, sew down 2 sides. (Overlock seams with zigzag if using woven material.)

With seams of pocket inside, sew one top edge to lining (i.e. you now put the inner flap pocket inside the knitted bag, between the knitted piece and the lining pocket which is in the centre of the bag). This join with the lining must be neat; you can turn over a little hem so that the sewing will not be seen. Now cover this with a strip of snap or popper tape, which you sew to both sides of tapestry material pocket. Bind all visible seams.

Repeat for the other tapestry pocket on the opp side of bag.

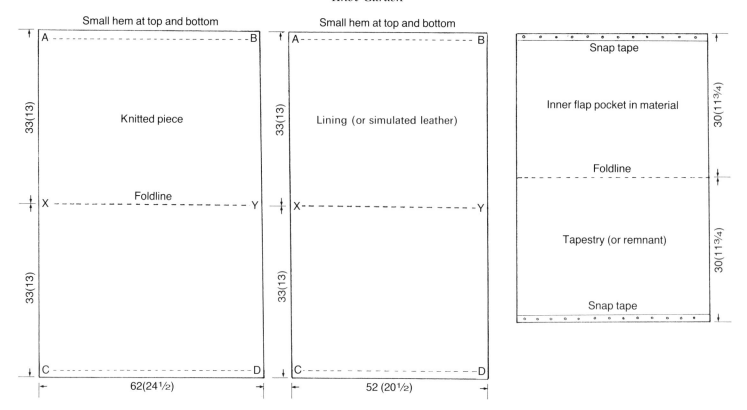

Small hem at top and bottom

A - B

33(13)

Knitted piece

Foldline

X - - - - - - - - - - Foldline - - - - - - - - - Y

33(13)

C - D

62(24½)

Small hem at top and bottom

A - B

33(13)

Lining (or simulated leather)

X - Y

33(13)

C - D

52 (20½)

Snap tape

Inner flap pocket in material

30(11¾)

Foldline

Tapestry (or remnant)

30(11¾)

Snap tape

115 Knot garden measurements

· **A**TTACHING SMALL POCKETS ·

Attach 3 small pockets to each end of the bag, sewing them down to the RS of work. Sew small buttons to pocket flaps, which are turned to RS along folding lines.

· **FINISHING OFF** ·

Sew press fasteners to the 3 clasps and to the opposite side of the bag to correspond. Sew large buttons to cover poppers on clasps. Attach handle to both sides of bag, at a length that is comfortable to hang over your shoulder.

· **V**ARIATIONS ON THE DESIGN ·

If you like the shape of the bag, but would prefer not to have the intarsia design, you could knit yourself a nautical-style bag.

Use 100 per cent cotton indigo, which is a cotton that fades with washing. You could knit the bag plain and then decorate it with nautical motifs; or you could knit a cowboys' bag, using leather fringing and scrolled buckles and clasps. A rope handle would look good with this bag.

If you knitted the shape of the bag in a white cotton, you could decorate the sides of the bag with bright embroidery, and have clusters of French knots scattered over the knitting.

· French knots ·

Bring the thread out at the required position, hold the thread down with the left thumb and encircle the thread twice with the needle. Still holding it firmly, twist the needle back to the starting point, and insert it close to where the thread first emerged. Pull it through to the back and secure for a single knot, or pass on to the position of the next stitch for a cluster.

This could be decorated with brightly-coloured wooden beads. You could knit a length of any coloured knitting and then cut out different shapes from this and sew down, having turned in a little hem on your knitted shape.

EVENING TOP DESIGNS

The designs for evening tops use embroidery and bead-work. The design in Fig 116a has cut-out shoulders which are edged in ribbon. Fig 116b has different textures, and a ribbon threaded through; Fig 116c has knitted flowers and embroidery, and Fig 116d shows beads knitted on by hand and on the machine.

To a plain knitted background there are many ways in which you can add a luxury touch.

Gathered ribbon around the welt is pretty. Work one or two rows of running stitching along a length of ribbon. Draw up the threads to fit around the welt, and slipstitch the ribbon in place, just under the frilled edge.

To make a ruched ribbon, measure and mark 2.5cm (1in) intervals along the ribbon length. Work diagonal lines of stitching from point to point. Draw up the threads and secure the ends.

116 Designs for evening sweaters

117 *Oakleaf jacket – reeds and hedgerow*

OAKLEAF JACKET

· machine-knitted jacket ·

The jacket was inspired by seeing a landscape of fields, hedgerows and trees, and then reducing it to a geometric outline of horizontal lines with blocks of colour.

You can see in Fig 119 how an outline of a tractor with a sprayer attached can be reduced to vertical and horizontal lines.

Verticals and horizontals used in the same design give a very forceful impression (*Fig 117*). The weeds and reeds, drawn on a windy day in May, illustrate what happens when a vertical line is crossed by a horizontal. The horizontal line in the sketch is the hedgerow. The eye is drawn upward by the strong vertical line of the reeds, but as soon as the hedgerow crosses that line, the movement is stopped.

Any sort of curve is also compelling, but in a much softer way. The sketch of the wind pattern on a field of grass (*Fig 118*) was made on the same day as the reeds, and shows the extraordinary rhythmical movement the wind makes. On the pattern, this is interpreted by tucked pattern B.

The jacket knitted as suggested would look perfect with a long black skirt. It is an easy design for all figure shapes to wear.

· DESIGN ·

This jacket is machine-knitted on a Chunky 120. The jacket has a stand-up collar, and a wide, full yoke that gathers into the waist. It has a peplum that fits smoothly over the hips. The sleeves have an unusual puff at the top and wrist, and incorporate several techniques that are fun for the creative machine knitter to try out.

· SIZE ·

To fit up to 91cm (36in) bust.

· MATERIALS ·

Yarns by Rowan
630g (22oz) Botany, cream, shade 1, col A
275g (10¼oz) fine cotton chenille, shade 386, col B
200g (7¼oz) Botany, deep pink, shade 96, col C
250g (9oz) Botany, blue, shade 55, col D
125g (4¾oz) Botany, peacock, shade 125, col E
250g (9oz) Botany, emerald green, shade 124, col F
250g (9oz) Botany, lime green, shade 34, col G
200g (7¼oz) Botany, pale green, shade 76, col H
125g (4¾oz) Botany, purple, shade 99, col I
8 small, 1 large, oakleaf porcelain buttons
9 press fasteners
Approx 18 long, 18 short, beads
7mm (¼in) elastic for waist
Cotton tape to stabilize shoulder seams
1m (39in) cream braid

· PATTERN NOTES ·

Use 3 strands of Botany wool together, and 1 end of chenille.

The yoke back is knitted from side to side, rather than from waist upward. The two front yokes are also knitted sideways, from the side to the front band. The peplum pieces are knitted upwards, from hem to waist.

The patterns on the front pieces do not match, as they continue over the shoulder on the back piece; so when the instruction is given to 'reverse shapings', you reverse the shaping, rather than the needles, for blocks of different colours within the pattern.

119 Oakleaf jacket design

118 Oakleaf jacket – wind patterns

· TENSION ·

19 sts and 28 rs to 10cm (4in) measured over st st (T5.1 approx).

· PATTERN A ·

A pattern in blocks of colours worked over 76 sts (ns to 36, left of centre 0, and ns to 40, right of centre 0 in WP).

In B, K 1 r, in C, K 4 rs, in B, K 1 r. Lift patt knob; side and front levers forward.

Pull ns 16, 17, 20 and 21 left of centre 0, and ns 1, 2, 5, 6, 19, 20, 23 and 24 right of centre 0 to E position. In G, K 1 r. Bring the same ns again to E position.

Pull ns 19, 18, 15 and 14 left of centre 0, and 3, 4, 7, 8, 21, 22, 25, and 26 right of centre 0 to E position. In F, K 1 r. Bring the same ns again to E position. In F, K 1 r.

Pull ns 1–13 and 22–36, both inclusive, left of centre 0, and ns 9–18 and 27–40, both inclusive, right of centre 0 to

E position. In A, K 1 r. Pull out the same ns again to E position. In A, K 1 r.

Side levers back. In H, K 2 rs. Side levers forward. Bring ns 0–36 left of centre 0 to E position. In D, K 1 r. Bring the same ns again to E position. In D, K 1 r. Bring all ns right of centre 0 to E position. In I, K 1 r. Bring the same ns again to E position. In I, K 1 r.

Side levers back. In A, K 2 rs. Side levers forward. All ns left of centre 0, and up to, and including, 19 on right, to E position. In I, K 1 r. Bring the same ns again to E position. In I, K 1 r.

Bring ns 20–40, right of centre 0, to E position. In E, K 1 r. Bring the same ns again to E position. In E, K 1 r. Side levers back. In A K 10 rs.

· PATTERN B ·

A tucking pattern.

In I, K 2 rs; in C, K 4 rs. From 6 rs down, pick up the loops between ns 18 and 19, and ns 19 and 20 left of centre 0, and put on ns 18 and 19. Rep on the loops between sts on

Oakleaf Jacket

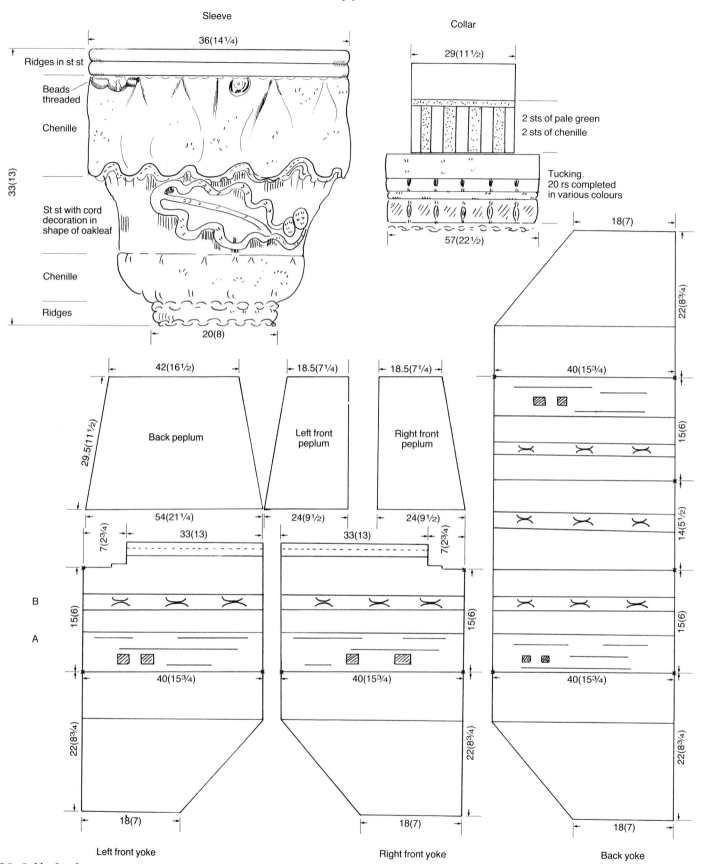

Sleeve

36(14¼)

Ridges in st st

Beads threaded

Chenille

33(13)

St st with cord decoration in shape of oakleaf

Chenille

Ridges

20(8)

Collar

29(11½)

2 sts of pale green
2 sts of chenille

Tucking.
20 rs completed in various colours

57(22½)

18(7)

22(8¾)

40(15¾)

15(6)

14(5½)

15(6)

42(16½)

29.5(11½)

Back peplum

54(21¼)

18.5(7¼)

Left front peplum

24(9½)

18.5(7¼)

Right front peplum

24(9½)

7(2¾)

33(13)

33(13)

7(2¾)

B

15(6)

A

X

40(15¾)

40(15¾)

15(6)

X

40(15¾)

22(8¾)

18(7)

22(8¾)

18(7)

22(8¾)

18(7)

Left front yoke

Right front yoke

Back yoke

120 *Oakleaf jacket measurements. The sleeve shows various reductions in width and changes in texture. Blocks of colour = Pattern A; Tucking pattern = Pattern B*

136

ns 20 and 21, and 21 and 22 left of centre 0, and put on ns 22 and 23.

Rep for loops between ns at 0 and 1, and 1 and 2 left of centre, and put on ns 3 and 4 left of centre 0. Put loops between ns at 0 and 1, and 1 and 2 right of centre, and put on ns 1 and 2 right of centre.

Rep on loops surrounding n 20 right of centre 0, as described for left side of centre. Bring out these 12 ns (3 groups of 4 ns with 2 loops on each st) to E position, to make it easier for the machine.

· BACK YOKE ·

COn in WY over ns 6 to 40 on right of centre 0. (34 sts). K several rs, change to A.

RC000. T5.1. K 2 rs. Cont in st st, *at the same time*, on left of work, inc 1 st on ev r, i.e. with 2-prong transfer tool, move the 2 end sts 1 n out, pick up the loop below the st just moved to the left to make a st, place it on the empty n, and bring these 3 ns to E position to make it easier for the machine.

Inc thus until there are 76 sts on machine. K straight until RC62. Mark both ends of r.

RC000. K patt A (16 rs). In A, K 10 rs. K patt B (6 rs). In A, K 10 rs. Mark right edge of work (for neck) *.

In A, K 16 rs. K 6 rs of patt B. In A, K 16 rs. Mark right edge of work (for neck). K 10 rs. K patt B. In A, K 10 rs. K patt A. Mark both ends of work.

RC000. In A, K 20 rs straight. *At the same time*, on left edge dec 1 st on ev r, i.e. with 2-prong transfer tool, move 2 end sts 1 st to the right. RC62. You will have 34 sts on machine. Release on several rows of WK.

· RIGHT FRONT YOKE ·

COn and K just as for back until *.

· Neck shaping ·

Carr at right. RC000. CO 10 sts at beg of next r, and K to end. Carr at left. K to right. CO 4 sts at beg of next r. K 6 rs straight. Mark left edge of knitting (14 sts dec).

· Right front border ·

In A, T3.3, K 8 rs. T10, K 1 r. T3.3, K 8 rs. Release on several rs of WK.

· LEFT FRONT YOKE ·

COn and K as for back, reversing shapings, until *.

· Neck shaping ·

RC000. In A, K 1 r to left. CO 10 sts at beg of next r, and K to end. Carr at right. K to left. CO 4 sts at beg of next r and K to end. Carr at right. K 6 rs. Mark right edge of knitting.

· Left front border ·

K as for right front border.

· BACK PEPLUM ·

In A, COn over 102 ns with a closed edge COn (by hand method) K 2 rs. Carr on right.

RC000. A, T5.1, K in st st, *at the same time*, dec with 3-prong transfer tool, 1 st at each end of ev 7th r until there are 80 sts on machine. K straight to RC82. Release with several rs of WK.

· LEFT FRONT PEPLUM ·

In A, T5.1, COn over 46 sts with a closed edge COn. K 2 rs. Carr on right.

RC000. K in st st, *at the same time*, dec 1 st at left edge of ev 7th r until 35 sts on machine. K straight to RC82. Release as for back.

· RIGHT FRONT PEPLUM ·

As for left, but reversing shapings.

· SLEEVES (*2 alike*) ·

· Sleeve puff (*knitted separately*) ·

Bring 102 ns to WP. Cast on 'e' loop method in A. K 4 rs. In B, K 24 rs. Release on several rs of WK.

Join shoulders.

· Sleeve ·

Open out work, WS facing you. Bring up 68 ns to WP. Rehang sts from armhole onto ns, with shoulder seam at centre 0.

RC000. T5.1. In C, K 12 rs. Using single-hole transfer tool, pick up loops of the sts 8 rs down and place them onto the ns. In I, K 12 rs.

Using single-hole transfer tool, pick up the loops of the sts 8 rs down and place them onto the needles. In addition to the 2 sts now on each n, replace sts from the CO end of sleeve puff (this is the work in chenille just completed) *with right side of puff facing you*, and with 2 sts on ev 2nd n (i.e. you will now have 3 sts on n 1, 4 sts on n 2, 3 sts on n 4, 4 sts on n 4, along the line of ns).

CO so that you are left with only B in each n. To do this, sl the 2 sts in I behind the n latch, and pull through the 1 or 2 sts on the n in B. Pull out all ns to E position.

· Thread up beads ·

Attach one end of a length of yarn in I to RS of work. Thread a short bead: the bead passes under 2 ns, the thread goes over 1 n. Now thread a long bead (alternatively you can use big and small beads; it's more attractive to change the appearance of the beads along the line of knitting); the long bead spans the width of 4 ns. Pass the length of I over 1 n, then thread up another short (or small) bead, and so on, along the width of knitting. Leave the thread loose; you can tighten it later when you have knitted the row.

Using just 2 strands of I, K back 1 r by hand, then CO (the beaded thread wil be incorporated in this row).

· Sleeve ruff (*knitted separately*) ·

COn in WK over 51 ns. Change to B, T5.1, K 12 rs. Release on several rs of WK.

· Cuff (*knitted from wrist end upwards*) ·

In C, COn 'e' loop over 34 ns. RC000. T5.1, K 2 rs. Change to I, K 12 rs. Using single-hole transfer tool, pick up the loops of the sts 8 rs down and place them onto the ns. In I, K 1 r.

With RS of separately-knitted sleeve ruff facing you, replace onto ns (i.e. ev 2nd n will have 2 sts of B replaced onto it). With length of I, CO r of sts by hand, as described before (i.e. the st in I is slipped behind latch, the sts in B are pulled through). Now turn the work just CO.

Push up 34 ns to WP. With WS of sleeve ruff facing you, replace the sts from the last r knitted in B onto ns (i.e. ev 2nd n will have 2 sts in it). T5.1, with C, K 34 rs. Release on WY. Turn the work just completed. Replace sts onto the ns.

With WS of sleeve puff facing you (this is the work that was knitted down on garment piece), replace now the sts from the last r knitted in B, before WK. (You will replace onto the needles with 3 sts in B, onto 1 st in C, so work will now have 4 sts in each n.)

Now push back all these sts behind the n latches, and with a length of C, CO the r by hand. (The WK on the work in B is left on at this point as a decorative effect.)

· POCKET ·

Push up 20 ns to WP. With RS of garment facing you, and picking up from waist end of right front yoke piece, replace 20 sts from a r of knitting in I. (Pick up from 2nd r knitted in I, just before that knitted in C.) Pull these ns out to E position.

RC000. T5.1. In I, K 14 rs. Now pick up the loops between sts from 4 rs down. With F, K 2 rs. Change to D, K 4 rs. Again, pick up loops between sts from 4 rs down. In H, K 2 rs. T10, K 1 r (fold line). T5.1, K 3 rs. Take off on WY.

· GATHERS (*4 alike*) ·

These are used as a decorative effect on the fronts, but are optional. With H, COn with 'e' loop method over 18 sts. T5.1, K 2 rs. Carr on right. With B, K 12 rs. Take off on WY.

· CORDS (*2 alike*) ·

These are used as a raised decorative outline on cuffs. With 2 strands only of C, COn over 3 sts. T4.1, K 140 rs. CO.

· PEPLUM FRONT BORDERS ·
· *(left and right the same)* ·

Push up 56 ns to WP. WS of work facing, latch up from the straight edge of front peplum onto ns. Bring up 1 n at each end to make a st.

In H, T3.3, K 8 rs. T10, K 1 r (fold row). T3.3, K 8 rs. Release on several rs of WK.

· BOBBLES (4 *alike*) ·

With C, T5.1, COn by hand over 9 sts. K 7 rs. With a length of C, thread through sts on machine and take off, then thread through 3 rem sides on bobble, pull up, and fasten.

· COLLAR ·

· Ruff ·

Push up 108 ns. With a length of G, COn by hand. RC000. T5.1, K 3 rs. Carr on left. Counting from left edge, pull out ev 5th n to HP.

Front levers back. In I, K 4 rs. Carr on left. Pattern knob up, right side lever and front levers forward. In D, K 1 r. Right side lever back. In H, K 6 rs. Pick up the loops of the sts 5 rs down and place them onto the ns. K to left.

Pull out ev 5th n to HP. Front levers back. In D, K 4 rs. Carr on left. Pattern knob up, right side lever and front levers forward. In I, K 1 r. (RC20). Right side lever back. K 6 rs in C. Release on several rs of WK.

· Stand-up collar ·

Push up 54 ns to WP. WS of ruff facing, return sts from work just completed, returning sts from last r in C, just before WK (2 sts to 1 n). Mark st on n 27 for collar centre.

RC000. T6, in C, K 2 rs. Change to H. Carr on right. * Pull the first 2 ns to E position, then leave 2 ns, then pull 2 out to E position, along the r. Pattern knob up, side and front levers forward. K to left. Again, pull out the same ns along the line of knitting to E position. K to right. Remove H without breaking the yarn, and change to B.

Now pull out to E position those ns that were not knitted in the previous 2 rs. K 1 r in B. Bring the same ns to E position. K 1 r in B. Remove yarn without breaking. * Carr on right.

With H and B, rep from * to * 4 more times (RC22). T6, side levers back, K to left in B.

· Picot row ·

Use single transfer tool and transfer from 1 st to next door; keep n in WP.

· Collar facing ·

In H, T5.1, K 13 rs straight (RC36). Release from machine with several rs of WK.

· MAKING UP ·

· Join back yoke and back peplum ·

Push up 78 ns to WP. Carr on left. With RS of back yoke facing you, loop up from waist edge, between markers; ease onto ns.

With WS facing you, replace sts from back peplum onto ns, from last r knitted in A so that you have 2 sts on each n. Pull ns to HP. In A, T5.1, K 1 r. CO.

· Join front yokes and front peplums ·

Push up 35 ns to WP. Carr on left. With RS of left front yoke facing you, loop up from waist edge, between markers.

With WS of left front peplum facing you, replace sts from last r of knitting in A onto ns, so that you have 2 sts on each n. Finish as for joining back yoke and peplum. Repeat for right front yoke and right front peplum.

Measure your waist and subtract 2.5cm (1in). Cut a length of elastic to this measurement and hem to waist seam on inside.

Steam collar ruff to flatten edging. Mark centre on garment back, and place collar marker at this point, WS of collar to RS of back neck on garment. Front collar meets at markers on right and left yoke. Sew collar to garment pieces, along this line, then fold collar facing to inside. Sew down the two collar side edges, then along neck seam.

Cut tape to length from sleeve top to sleeve top, and catch down to seam that extends from shoulder, along back neck to the other shoulder. Sew all seams.

Fold front yoke bands and front peplum bands to inside, along fold line, and catch down. Try on garment to find the length on the peplum you want. Turn a hem to inside, easing in neatly; tack and then hem. Fold pocket facing to inside, hem down.

On gathers, pull a length of B through sts on r before WK, and pull up to approx 4cm (1¾in). Sew 2 in a fan shape at waist on both fronts, catching down edges.

Sew braid along both front bands. Sew on press

fasteners, 8 along right front bands, and 1 to the inside of the pocket, at the middle. Sew buttons on top of fasteners, the large button going at the waist.

Sew a large oakleaf shape on the knitting in C on both sleeves; allow a short length for a stalk, and position 2 bobbles on end of stalk.

· STITCH PATTERN VARIATIONS ·

The fabric for a knitted jacket should be firm. The examples in Fig 121 of various stitch patterns would all be suitable for this design.

The first sketch shows a jacket with a buttoned pocket, ribbed inset on the sleeves, and a short knitted cape attached at the collar line.

It has a negative/positive patterning, using Brother pattern card 15D, and is knitted in 2/8 Shetland wool, working 20 rows of Fair Isle pattern striped with 6 rows of stocking stitch. The darker-coloured yarn is used as background and striping colour on the peplum, as this has the effect of reducing bulky areas.

The second sketch illustrates a lovely tendril chain stitch decoration worked over knitting to give a tapestry appearance to the jacket. This is a double-bed stitch pattern, knitted on a Passap Duomatic 80. 3 strands of a fine lambswool were used together; the needle set-up is shown in Diag 10.

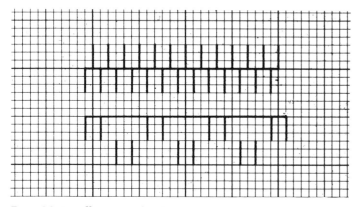

Diag 10 Needle set-up for double-bed stitch pattern

Handle down
Orange strippers
T4.3/4.2
2 rs N/AX←
2 rs N/AX 0
Rep

This style is worn over a full flared skirt in cream antique lace, and was knitted in jade green with dark navy decoration.

The third sketch shows a very textured stitch. On the sleeves it is used with the purl side of the knitting used on the right side. This is a lovely ripple stitch made by setting the machine so that it won't knit those stitches in HP.

Pull out every 10th needle to HP, * knit 4 rows (you are tucking on those needles in HP). Knit 2 rows, all stitches. Again, pull out every 10th needle to HP, knit 4 rows. Knit 2 rows all stitches. Now, with the single transfer tool, pick up the whole collection of stitches from the first rows of tuck, and lift them onto that needle. K 1 row to the left. Along the line of knitting, now pull out the 5th, and every following 10th needle, so that the new needles tucking are equidistant between those needles tucking before.

The machine must be set so that it won't knit back those needles in HP, and two repeats of tuck are worked on each set of needles. This produces a very pronounced tuck in a diamond shape.

The last design has a flounced collar, and a ribbed inset on either side of the waist to pull in the gathers. There is a shawl-effect collar which ties at the front.

A velvety material would be ideal for the jacket, such as chenille and velour yarns. Or you could boil Shetland wool, which produces a felted effect. *Felting* is a process that occurs to the Shetland wool during the washing cycle. Either rub the knitting hard while hand washing or put a long length of fabric into the washing machine. On your hottest cycle, boiled at 95 degrees, a felt is produced that is very warm and quite weather-proof.

Use luxury yarns such as angora, cashmere and alpaca blends, using a small pattern motif, rather than a large one. This style of jacket, with its puffed sleeves and gathered-in yoke, can be decorated and added to, to great effect. It is a romantic-style jacket, so feel free to create a rich, embossed appearance.

121 Oakleaf jacket – changing stitch pattern

SUPPLIERS — UK

· MAIL ORDER YARNS ·

Atkinson Yarn Designer Collection
Terry Mills
Ossett
West Yorkshire
WF5 9SA

Falcon-by-post
Falcon Mills
Bartle Lane
Bradford
West Yorkshire

French Wools Ltd
7–11 Lexington Street
London
W1R 4BU

Holmfirth Wools Ltd
Briggate
Windhill
Shipley
West Yorkshire
BD18 2BS

Nethy Products
22 Dunlop Street
Stewarton
Kilmarnock
KA3 5AS

Nina A. Miklin
104 Biddulph Mansion
Elgin Avenue
Maida Vale
London
W9 1HU

Pamela Wise
101–105 Goswell Road
London
EC1V 7DH

Rowan Yarns
Green Lane Mill
Washpit
Holmfirth
West Yorkshire

Texere Yarns
College Mill
Barkerend Road
Bradford
BD3 9AQ

· BUTTONS ·

(*Porcelain buttons designed by Carolyn Hird*)
Quox
The Old Brewery
Broughton Hall
Broughton
Skipton
N. Yorkshire

Mail order buttons:
Duttons
15 & 30 Lowther Arcade
Harrogate
HG1 1RZ

· DECORATIVE AND · · HABERDASHERY GOODS ·

Creative Beadcraft Ltd
Demark Works
Sheepcote Dell Road
Beamond End
Nr. Amersham
Bucks

S. Kersen Ltd
87–95 Cleveland Street
London
W1P 6JL

· MACHINE KNITTING GOODS ·

Metropolitan Sewing Machines
321 Ashley Road
Parkstone
Poole
Dorset
BH14 0AP

· LARGE GRID GRAPH PAPER, ·
· SPECIALIST DESIGN BOOKS, ETC. ·

R.D. Franks Ltd
Kent House
Market Place
Oxford Circus
London
W1N 8EJ

SUPPLIERS — US

· YARNS ·

American Thread Co.
High Ridge Park
Stamford
Connecticut 06905

Berga Ullman Inc.
59 Demond Avenue
N. Adams
Massachusetts 01247

Emile Bernat & Sons Co.
Depot and Mendon Street
Uxbridge
Massachusetts 01569

Brunswick Worsted Mills Inc
230 Fifth Avenue
New York
N Y 10001

Erdal Yarns Ltd
303 Fifth Avenue
Room 1109
New York
N Y 10016

Exquisicat
Exquisicat Imports
P O Box 6321
Richmond
Virginia 23230

Folklorico Yarn Co.
522 Ramona Street
Palo Alto
California 94 301

MacKnit Knitting Machine Centre
70 East Palisade Avenue
Englewood
New Jersey 07631

National Needlework Association
National Hand Knitting Yarn Committee
230 Fifth Avenue
New York
N Y 10001

Needlecraft Corp. of America
3900 N. Claremont Avenue
Chicago
Illinois 60618

Plymouth Yarn Company
500 Lafayette Street
Bristol
Pennsylvania 19007

William Unger & Co.
230 Fifth Avenue
New York
N Y 10001

· MACHINE INFORMATION ·

Knitting Machine Dealers Ass.
222–15 Braddock Avenue
Queens Village
New York
N Y 11428

INDEX